# *Accidental Death of an Anarchist*

## *by Dario Fo*

### *Adapted by Richard Nelson*

Based on a literal translation by Suzanne
Cowan, with editing by Ron Jenkins and
Joel Schechter.

Originally Produced on Broadway by
Alexander H. Cohen

# SAMUEL FRENCH, INC.
45 WEST 25TH STREET      NEW YORK 10010
7623 SUNSET BOULEVARD      HOLLYWOOD 90046
*LONDON*      *TORONTO*

## IMPORTANT BILLING & CREDIT REQUIREMENTS

All producers of ACCIDENTAL DEATH OF AN ANARCHIST *must* give credit to Dario Fo and original author of the Play and Richard Nelson as the translator and adaptor in all programs distributed in connection with performances of the Play, and in all instances in which the title of the Play appears for the purposes of advertising, publicizing or otherwise exploiting the Play and/or a production thereof, including, without limitation to, programs, souvenir books and playbills. The names of Dario Fo and Richard Nelson *must* also appear on separate lines on which no other matter appears, immediately following the title of the play, in substantially the following format:

(Name of Producer)
presents

ACCIDENTAL DEATH OF AN ANARCHIST

By

DARIO FO
adapted by
RICHARD NELSON

# BELASCO THEATRE

🎭 A Shubert Organization Theatre

Gerald Schoenfeld, *Chairman*　　　　　　　　　　　Bernard B. Jacobs, *President*

---

ALEXANDER H. COHEN and HILDY PARKS
present

## Accidental Death of an Anarchist

by
### DARIO FO

adapted by
### RICHARD NELSON

starring
### JONATHAN PRYCE

and
(alphabetically)

### GERRY BAMMAN　　JOE GRIFASI　　BILL IRWIN
### PATTI LuPONE　　RAYMOND SERRA

Casting by
MEG SIMON / FRAN KUMIN

| Scenic Design by | Lighting Design by | Costume Design by | Hair Design by |
|---|---|---|---|
| KARL EIGSTI | ALLEN LEE HUGHES | PATRICIA ZIPPRODT | JOSEPH DAL CORSO |

Co-Producer
BERNARD GERSTEN

General Manager
MARTHA MASON

Directed by
## DOUGLAS C. WAGER

This adaptation originally produced by
Arena Stage, Washington, D.C.
The Producers and Theatre Management are Members of
The League of New York Theatres and Producers, Inc.

## CAST

*(in order of appearance)*

The Fool ..................................... JONATHAN PRYCE

The Sergeant ..................................... BILL IRWIN

Inspector Bertozzo .............................. GERRY BAMMAN

Captain Pisani ..................................... JOE GRIFASI

Chief Bellati ................................. RAYMOND SERRA

The Reporter ................................... PATTI LuPONE

### ACT ONE

Scene 1: Rome, Italy — Central Police Headquarters
2nd Floor Office

Scene 2: The same building, 4th Floor Office

### ACT TWO

Later that day.

*THERE WILL BE ONE FIFTEEN-MINUTE INTERMISSION*

STANDBYS AND UNDERSTUDIES
Standbys and understudies never substitute for listed players unless a specific
announcement for the appearance is made at the time of the performance.

Standby for MR. PRYCE—SETH ALLEN
Standby for MR. IRWIN and MR. BAMMAN—ROBERT FITCH

Understudy for Chief Bellati and Captain Pisani—FRANK BIANCAMANO;
for The Reporter—MAIA DANZIGER.

## A Note on the Text of
## ACCIDENTAL DEATH OF AN ANARCHIST

CHIEF. . . . the officer was referring to the first version. We're talking about the second one.

FOOL. Ah, that's right. . . . Let's hear it: what did you correct?

Like the police transcripts discussed in the play, the play itself has been altered a number of times since its first production in Italy in 1970. The version printed in this volume was first created by Richard Nelson in 1983 for a production at Arena Stage. His adaption was based on Suzanne Cowan's literal translation, published in *Theater* Magazine in 1979. For the Arena Stage production and the subsequent Broadway production, both directed by Douglas Wager, Nelson revised the dialogue for the American stage, and added some references to current politics. His adaptation was approved by Dario Fo. Subsequently, Fo asked for further changes in the text, which were made by Ron Jenkins and Joel Schechter, in collaboration with Fo and Franca Rame. The changes include some new political references, and dialogue closer in meaning to that of the original Italian text. These changes were made with the consent of Richard Nelson, who remains credited as the American adaptor of the play. Future productions of the text may require further alteration of political references, unless our President is elected for a life term, and outlives the century.

ACCIDENTAL DEATH OF AN ANARCHIST was first staged on December 5, 1970, in Varese (Lombardy), Italy.

Richard Nelson's adaptation, directed by Doug Wager, opened at Arena Stage in Washington, D.C., on Feb. 9, 1984.

# PROLOGUE

On the night of December 12, 1969, a bomb exploded and killed sixteen people at the Agricultural Bank in Milan. At the same time, another bomb exploded at a bank in Rome, which did not go by without causing casualties, and another bomb was discovered at the tomb of the unknown soldier. Milan police arrested an anarchist, Guiseppe Pinelli, and accused him of the crime. At a certain point in his interrogation, the anarchist flew out the window of the police station. The same day, another anarchist — a dancer by profession — was arrested; he was suspected of being the one really responsible for the bomb in Milan.

Something similar occurred in New York in 1921, when the anarchist Salsedo flew out the window of a police station, around the same time that Sacco and Vanzetti were arrested for a crime never proven against them. Their story has nothing to do with the one we are telling now. But from these stories we can conclude that many anarchists are obsessed by the urge to jump out of the window, because they believe they are able to fly.

It is an illusion of theirs that when they're two or three yards from the ground, they merely have to open their arms and move their feet to fly up again. Some observers have suspected that anarchists are able to fly, but they are also so underhanded that they smash themselves to the ground, just to incriminate the police and other state institutions by dying.

Anyway, the investigation of the death of the anarchist in Milan was (filed away in the archives.) The dancer anarchist was proven innocent after three years in jail. Public pressure has frequently been exerted on authorities to re-open the investigation of the anarchist Pinelli's death in Milan, but they keep postponing it.

# Accidental Death of an Anarchist

## ACT ONE

### SCENE 1

*A normal room in central police headquarters. A desk,
   large cabinet, some chairs, a typewriter, a telephone,
   two doors, an open window.*
*From the window we hear a large angry crowd.*
*SUSPECT sits calmly in front of the desk. SERGEANT
   stands near the window, looking out, though careful
   not to show himself to the mob. Pause.*

SUSPECT. The demonstrators appear to be rather tense
today.

SERGEANT. More than tense. I would say they've been
incited.

SUSPECT. By whom?

SERGEANT. The unions. Those people in the streets
are workers on to protest that they've been fired or
evicted.

SUSPECT. And why do they always demonstrate here
at police headquarters? Right here, under the main
window?

SERGEANT. It's always the same story. We're always
caught in-between. It's only one week since that anarchist we were interrogating jumped out the window.

SUSPECT. That window? But it's only two stories up.

SERGEANT. Another window—upstairs. On the fourth floor. (*He walks away from the window.*)

SUSPECT. Oh.

(*THE INSPECTOR hurries in, with a file in his hands.*)

INSPECTOR. (*entering*)
My apologies. I'm running a bit behind this morning. Sergeant, what the hell is that window doing opened?

SERGEANT. I'm sorry, inspector. (*He goes and closes the window—noise ends.*)

SUSPECT. The room seemed a little stuffy.

SERGEANT. I wasn't talking to you. Just sit down and shut up.

INSPECTOR. (*going through file*) Now let's go to your problem. It's obvious from your record that this isn't the first time you've been arrested for disguise. I see you've passed yourself off twice as a surgeon . . . true or false?

SUSPECT. You should know how thin the line is between truth and lies, inspector.

INSPECTOR. (*upset*) Please! Once as a pediatrician. . . .

SUSPECT. (*to SERGEANT*) Can I help it if I like kids?

INSPECTOR. . . . three times as a bishop, once as a naval engineer. . . . So in all you've been arrested— two and one are . . . three. Three and . . .

SUSPECT. Would it help if I loaned you my calculator? (*INSPECTOR takes out a Chinese abacus and quickly adds up the sum.*)

INSPECTOR. No thank you. It comes to . . . eleven times. And this makes twelve. What do you have to say for yourself?

SUSPECT. Yes, twelve arrests, but please notice that I've never been convicted. My record is clean.

INSPECTOR. I guarantee we will mess it up this time. The indictment states that you impersonated a psychiatrist, professor from the University of Padova. Don't you know you could go to jail for assuming a position under false pretenses?

SUSPECT. A sane person could, but I couldn't. I am licensed to be crazy. See here, I have my complete clinical file with me. Sixteen times institutionalized — and always for the same reason: "histromania": from the Latin 'histrones', which means, of course, "actor". See, I can't stop myself from playing roles — and as you can tell I've already developed a rather rich repertory. Of course, inside a theater this would be considered quite normal, but unfortunately I am more into real-life acting and I draw my company from real people — who don't know they're playing roles. Which, by the way, is a good thing, as I don't have the money to pay them. I did apply for a grant from the National Endowment for the Arts, but unfortunately Reagan cut the whole budget for dance and theater. An actor who hates the theater. It's terrible.

INSPECTOR. So you are supported by your actors. You have them by the neck.

SUSPECT. I don't have to do anything. They're just always there when I need them.

INSPECTOR. It says here you actually charged a hundred thousand lire for one appointment.

SERGEANT. What a con man!

SUSPECT. The normal fee for any self-respecting psychiatrist . . . for one who has studied the same profession for sixteen years.

INSPECTOR. Fine, but when did you ever study anything?

SUSPECT. Why, I studied for twenty years in sixteen different mental institutions, examining thousands of insane people like myself, day after day . . . and at night too. Because I, unlike normal psychiatrists, slept with them — sometimes standing up with two others, because there are never enough beds. Anyway, look into the matter, and you'll see if I didn't make an absolutely perfect diagnosis of that poor schizophrenic, the one I was indicted for.

INSPECTOR. The twenty thousand lire were absolutely perfect too!

SUSPECT. But Inspector, I had to charge him that much, for his own good!

INSPECTOR. Ah, for his own good. It was part of the treatment?

SUSPECT. Of course. If I hadn't taken that twenty thousand from him, do you suppose that poor man, and especially his family, would have been satisfied? If I had charged him five thousand, they undoubtedly would have thought, "This must be a second-rate doctor, maybe not even a real M.D.; he's probably just out of medical school, a beginner." This way, instead, as soon as he received my bill they were all dumb-founded. They wondered: who on earth can this be? The eternal father? and went off as happy as larks. They even kissed my hand . . . "Thanks so much, doctor" . . . and wept with emotion.

INSPECTOR. You really know how to tell a story.

SUSPECT. But these aren't fibs, Inspector. Even Freud said that tidy fees are the most effective remedy, both for the doctor and the patient!

INSPECTOR. I believe it! Anyway, take a look at your professional card and prescription list. If I'm not mistaken, they read: "Professor Antonio A. Antonio, Psychiatrist. The Former Professor. University of Padova." Go on, what do you have to say now?

SUSPECT. First of all, I really am a professor. Professor

of drawing, ornate and free-hand styles, at the Holy Redeemer night school.

INSPECTOR. Well, isn't that nice. Good for you, but it says here, "Psychiatrist!"

SUSPECT. Yes, but after the period! Don't you know anything about syntax and punctuation? Look carefully: Professor Antonio A. Antonio. Period. Then there's a capital P. Psychiatrist. Now, you'll admit it isn't acting under false pretenses to say: "I am a psychiatrist." It's like saying, "I'm a psychologist, botanist, vegetarian, arthritic." Do you have a knowledge of Italian grammar and language? You do? Well, then you should know that if someone describes himself as an archaeologist, it's as though he had written "Milanese." It doesn't mean he has a degree in it!

INSPECTOR. All right, but what about that "The Former Professor from the University?"

SUSPECT. There, you see—excuse me, but this time you're the one who's acting under false pretenses: you told me that you know Italian language and syntax and punctuation, and then it comes out that you don't even read correctly.

INSPECTOR. What do you mean, I don't know—

SUSPECT. Didn't you see the comma after "The Former"?

INSPECTOR. Oh, yes, there is a comma. You're right, I hadn't noticed.

SUSPECT. Aha, "I hadn't noticed" . . . And you, simply because you "hadn't noticed," would throw an innocent man in prison?

INSPECTOR. You know, you really are crazy. (*Without realizing it, he has begun to address the SUSPECT in a more respectful tone.*) What does the comma have to do with it?

SUSPECT. Nothing, for someone who doesn't know

Italian language and syntax! Which reminds me, I'd like to know where you got your degree. And who granted it to you . . . let me finish! The comma, remember, is the key to everything! If there's a comma after "The Former," the entire meaning of the phrase changes at once. After the comma, you have to catch your breath . . . take a brief pause . . . Because "the comma always denotes a pause." Therefore, it should be read, "The Former, Professor," meaning, "the aforesaid, the one already mentioned, NOT the professor." In fact, I haven't been a professor for some time. So that could even be read with a little ironic chuckle: heh, heh. So the correct reading of that phrase is as follows: The Former, Professor, heh, heh. Pause. From the University of Padova. Just the same as if you read "retired dentist, from the city of Bergamo." Because I am from the University of Padova, in the sense that it was the last place I visited: I had just recently come from there when I, ah, took up my psychiatric practice. Any other reading of the phrase would be entirely false and misleading; only an idiot would make such an error.

INSPECTOR. So you think I'm an idiot!

SUSPECT. No, just ignorant of basic Italian grammar. But it's lucky for you you've come to the right person for help. I'll even offer a discount. I'll begin with the subordinates?

SERGEANT. Is he talking about me?

INSPECTOR. Quit putting me on! I'm beginning to think you really do have a mania for playing roles, but you're even playing the role of a nut. In fact, I'll bet you're even saner than I am.

SUSPECT. I wouldn't know. Certainly, your occupation is one which leads to many psychic alterations . . . let me examine your eye. (*He pulls down the INSPECTOR's lower eyelid with his thumb.*)

INSPECTOR. Look — just shut up and sit down so that we can get on with the report.

SUSPECT. Oh, good, I'll do the typing. I'm a certified at forty-five words a minute. Where do you keep the carbon?

INSPECTOR. Keep still or I'll handcuff you!

SUSPECT. You can't! Either the straightjacket or nothing. I'm insane, and if you put handcuffs on me — article 122 of the criminal code: "Anyone wearing the uniform of a public officer, who applies non-clinical or non-psychiatric instruments of restraint to a mentally disturbed individual, so as to cause an aggravation of said individual's condition, commits a crime punishable by five to fifteen years' imprisonment and the loss of his or her rank and pension."

INSPECTOR. Ah, I see you also have a background in law!

SUSPECT. Law? I know everything! I've been studying law for twenty years!

INSPECTOR. How old are you anyway, three hundred? Where did you study law?

SUSPECT. In mental hospitals! You have no idea how well one can study in there! There was a paranoid court reporter who coached me. What a genius! I know everything: Roman, modern, ecclesiastical law . . . the Justinian code . . . Federician, Lombard, Greek orthodox codes . . . everything! Try testing me.

INSPECTOR. As if I had time for that! But there's nothing here in your history about your being a judge . . . not even a lawyer?!

SUSPECT. Oh, no, I would never be a lawyer. I don't like to defend people; that's a passive occupation. I like to judge . . . sentence . . . repress . . . persecute! I fit right in with your kind of people, dear Inspector. Why don't we call each other by our first names?

INSPECTOR. Watch out, madman. You'd better go easy on the kidding.

SUSPECT. As you say.

INSPECTOR. Now then, have you ever impersonated a judge, or not?

SUSPECT. Ah — a judge! Now there you've touched a weak spot of mine, Inspector. That is indeed a noble profession: To judge! To sentence! To persecute! You're a police inspector, you must know the feeling. But being a judge is the best of all occupations. First of all you hardly ever have to retire. In fact, at the precise moment when an ordinary man, any working person, reaches fifty-five or sixty years old and already has to be dumped because he's beginning to get a little slow, a little late in his reflexes, the judge is just starting the high point of his career. A worker on the assembly line or cutting machine is washed up after the age of fifty; he causes slow-ups, accidents — he has to be gotten rid of! A fifty-five year old miner has silicosis: out, canned, fired, quickly before he can begin to draw his retirement pension. The same thing goes for bank tellers: at a certain age they begin to mess up the accounts, forget the names of companies and clients, discount rates, corporate executives — go home . . . scram . . . you're too old and feeble-minded! For judges, on the other hand, it's exactly the opposite: the older and more feeble-minded they get, the higher ranks they're promoted to. They're given important, absolute powers! You see a bunch of little old men, made out of cardboard and utterly incapable of moving their limbs; wearing satin cordons, ermine capes, shiny black top hats with golden stripes that make them look like bit players from the comic opera of Venice; doddering along with faces resembling small, dried Piedmontese mushrooms . . . pairs of spectacles hanging from their necks by little gold chains, otherwise they'd lose them; they can never remember where they put them down. Well, these characters have the power to save or destroy however and whenever they will: they toss out certain life sentences just the way someone might say, "hey, maybe it will rain tomorrow!" Fifty years for you . . . thirty for you . . . "You over there — twenty years!" "But I'm the prosecutor, your honor." "Oh, in that case, ten years." "You, five — I like your face." "Now, gentlemen, when I say three, make a deal. One. Two." Ah yes, yes indeed: judging is the occupation, the role I would give anything to play at least once in my life. The Supreme Court, the Superior Court judge — "your excellency; please be seated; silence, the court is coming in . . . oh, look I found a bone: is it yours? No, that's impossible; I have none left!"

INSPECTOR. Listen, will you cut out this blabbing!? You got me dizzy. Go on, sit down over there and shut up! (*He pushes him toward the chair.*)

SUSPECT. (*reacting hysterically*) Hey, hands off or I'll bite!

INSPECTOR. You'll bite who?

SUSPECT. You! I'll bite you on the neck and the buttock, too! Glom! And if you react with force there's article 122B: provocation and violence resulting in harm to a defenseless and disabled individual incapable of taking responsibility for his or her own actions. Six to nine years, and loss of your pension!

SERGEANT. What about rank?

SUSPECT. Ah, you can keep that.

INSPECTOR. Sergeant, I said . . . !

SERGEANT. But what if he bites me?

SUSPECT. Of course I'm going to bite you. And I have rabies too. I'm infectious. I got it from a dog: a rabid bastard hound who bit off half my ass. But he died and I recovered. I recovered, but I'm still infectious: Ggrrrmmmm! Oowowowowowoh!

INSPECTOR. Jesus Christ!

SUSPECT. Jesus? No, I was him last week.

INSPECTOR. Please, can't we just finish writing this report? If you're a good boy, I promise, I'll let you go.

SUSPECT. No, don't throw me out, Mr. Inspector. I'm so happy here with you, in the police . . . I feel protected; there are so many perils out there in the street. People are mean; they drive cars, honk their horns, step on squealing brakes . . . and they go on strike! There are buses and subway cars with big doors that snap shut . . . screeee, clak — squished! Keep me here with you. I'll help you make suspects talk . . . subversives too. I know how to make suppositories — with nitroglycerin.

INSPECTOR. Look, I'm just about fed up with you.

SUSPECT. Inspector, keep me here with you or I'll throw myself out the window. What floor are we on? Fourth? Well, it's almost standard practice: I'll jump! I'll jump, and when I'm lying down there dying, splattered all over the pavement and giving the death-rattle — . . . . I'll look up and say — it was him, the inspector! He threw me out. Inspector Bertozzo did! And I take a long time to die. I'm not fragile like the anarchist, who falls 4 floors and immediately goes into a coma after hitting the ground, so that he doesn't manage to tell the journalists anything. No, I will tell. The reporters will come and I'll tell them everything. I'm going to jump!

INSPECTOR. For god's sake, cut it out! (*to the PO-LICEMAN*) Lock the window. (*POLICEMAN obeys.*)

SUSPECT. Then I'll throw myself down the stairwell! (*heads for the door*)

INSPECTOR. Damn it! Now I've really had enough. Sit down! (*throws him onto the chair, to the cop*:) You lock that door . . . take out the key . . .

SUSPECT. and throw it out the window. (*Dazed, the POLICEMAN approaches the window.*)

SUSPECT. Right, throw it — NO, I mean put it in the strong box . . . lock the strong box . . . take out the key . . . (*The cop mechanically obeys.*)

SUSPECT. put it in your mouth and swallow it!

INSPECTOR. No, no, NO! Nobody's going to make a sucker out of me. (*to the cop*) Give me that key! (*opens the door*) Go on, get out . . . and throw yourself down the stairwell. Do what you want. Out! Get the hell out of here before they put me away!

SUSPECT. There's an idea — we could be roommates!

INSPECTOR. Out!

SUSPECT. No, Inspector . . . you can't! Don't act like a law-breaker. Don't shove, please! Why do you want me to get out? This isn't my stop!

INSPECTOR. Scram! (*He succeeds in pushing him out, then listens apprehensively for a moment at the door.*) Oh, finally!

POLICEMAN. Inspector, I should remind you that there's a meeting in Mr. Bellati's office, and we're already five minutes late.

INSPECTOR. Why, what time is it! (*Looks at his watch*) Oh, for crying out loud . . . that damn fool got me completely screwed up. Let's go, get a move on.

(*They exit from the left. On the right, the FOOL [SUS-PECT] sticks his head in the same door from which he had gone out.*)

FOOL. May I? Inspector . . . am I interrupting?

Don't get mad, I just came back to pick up my papers . . . How come you don't answer? Come on, you couldn't bear a grudge. Let's make up. Ah, there's nobody here! Well, I'll get them myself. My clinical report . . . prescription-list . . . hey, here's my criminal citation! Oh well, let's tear it up   out of sight, out of mind. Hm, wonder who this citation is for? (*reads*) "Armed robbery." In a pharmacy, that makes sense! It's all right, forget it, you're pardoned. (*tears up that citation also*) And what have you done? (*reads*) "Unlawful appropriation . . . damage . . . " Nonsense, nonsense. Go on, my boy, you're free! (*tears it up*) Everybody free! (*He stops to examine one particular document.*) No, not you, you bastard! You're staying right where you are . . . going up the river. (*He carefully smooths the document out on the table, and then opens the cabinet stuffed with files.*) Everybody freeze! The law has arrived. Wow, these couldn't all be criminal citations!? I'll burn the whole thing! A nice big bonfire! (*He takes out a cigarette lighter, starts to set fire to a large sheaf of documents, then reads on the cover.*) "Judicial inquiry in progress." (*then, on another folder*) "Order to file away transcript of judical inquiry." (*At that moment the telephone rings. The FOOL answers calmly.*) Hello, Inspector Bertozzo's office. Who's calling? No, I'm sorry but if you don't give your name I can't call him to the phone . . . What   Investigator   is it really you in person? No kidding, of things . . . What a pleasure! The defenstrating investigator! Nothing, nothing. And where are you calling from? Of course, how stupid of me; from the fourth floor — where else?

Tell me, what do you need to talk to Bertozzo about? No, he can't come to the phone, give me the message. A supreme court judge? They're sending him from

Washington? — oops, sorry, I mean from Rome; once in a while I forget about the theatrical transposition. Ah, he's supposed to be some kind of "auditor." Of course, apparently there's some disagreement within the Ministry of Justice, about the motivations of that judge who decided to have the investigation closed and filed away. But are you sure? Oh, it's just hearsay; that's what I figured. First they're delighted, then they get second thoughts. I see, because of the pressure of public opinion — oh, go on, public opinion. Pressure, hell. Exactly, Bertozzo is right here, snickering. (*He laughs, holding the receiver away from his face.*) Ha, ha! . . . and making obscene gestures . . . ha, ha! (*pretending to call out*) Bertozzo, our friend on the fourth floor says you can go ahead and laugh about it because you're not involved . . . but for him and his boss, it's a pain in the backside. Ha, ha! He says watch out when you wipe yourself! Ha, ha! No, this time it's me who's laughing. No, because I would really get a kick out of seeing the Head Commissioner caught up in it. Yeah, it's the truth; you can even tell him I said so. "Investigator Anghiari — that's me — would get a kick out of it" . . . Bertozzo agrees with me too; listen to him laughing. (*holds out the receiver*) Ha, ha! Hear that? And who gives a damn if we get shit thrown at us. Yeah, you can tell him that too: Anghiari and Bertozzo don't give a good goddam. (*lets out an enormous razzberry*) Prrrrttt. Yes, that was him giving the razzberry. But don't get hot under the collar: Good, that's better; we'll talk about it face to face. Now, what did you want from Bertozzo, which documents? Go ahead, I'm taking it down: copy of order to file away investigation of anarchist's death . . . O.K., and he should deliver it to you. Also copies of judicial transcripts. Right. Yes, it's all here in the files. I believe it!

You and the ex-warden of the concentration camp had
better get it together. If the judge who's on his way up
here is even a little bit of a bastard, like they say . . .
Sure I know the judge! Antonio A. Antonio, that's his
name. Never heard of him? Well, you will! He was in a
German concentration camp. Ask your boss if by any
chance . . . O.K., we'll send it all over to you right
away. So long. Wait a minute! Ha, ha    Bertozzo here
just made a really funny crack. Promise not to get mad
and I'll tell you what he said. You won't blow up? All
right, then, I'll tell you: he said    ha, ha!    as soon as that
judge-auditor winds up his visit here, you'll be sent down
south, maybe to the smallest backwater town in the pit of
Calabria, where central police headquarters consists of
one story and the inspector's office is in the sub-basement. Ha, ha! You get it? the sub-basement. Ha, ha! Ha,
ha, how'd you like that? You didn't like it? Well, better
luck next time. (*listens for a moment to voice on the
phone*) O.K., message received and transmitted.
Pprrrrttt! (*razzberry*) from both of us. Over and out! (*The
FOOL hangs up the phone and immediately launches
into a feverish search for the documents.*) Better get to
work, your honor the judge; time is pressing. God,
I'm so excited! It's as though I were about to take an
exam, more than one exam, for a Ph.D. from Oxford! If I
can convince them that I'm a real judge-auditor . . . if
they don't go wrong, hell, I've got it made! Let's see now;
first of all, got to find the right kind of walk. (*tries out a
slightly limping gait*) no, this is more like a court chan-
cellor's. An arthritic, but dignified step! Here, this is
more like it, with the neck a little twisted . . . like a very
old circus-horse. . . . (*tries it out and rejects it*) No,
there's an even better one: the "slide," with a little twitch

at the end. (*tries it*) Not bad at all! And the "pudding-knee?" (*tries it*) Or maybe the stiff-legged hopping one. (*tries it out: small, fast steps alternating heel-and-toe*) Gosh, what about glasses? No, no glasses . . . the right eye a bit closed . . . there, that's it, a wall-eyed expression, not much talk . . . A slight cough: hokk. No, no cough — maybe some tics? Well, we can think up a few on the spot, if necessary, a sugary manner, nasal voice?! Good-natured, but with sudden, sharp outbursts: "No! My dear chief, you have to stop it. You're not head warden of a fascist penitentiary any longer; you'd do well to remind yourself of that once in a while!" No, no, a completely opposite type would be better: cold, detached, commanding tone, monotonous voice; sad, somewhat nearsighted look . . . using glasses, but with only one lens, like this (*He does a quick rehearsal, at the same time leafing through some papers.*) Well, how do you like that! My god, the papers I was looking for, here they are right under my nose! Hey, calm down . . . musn't lose my cool like this; get back into character immediately. Attention, please! (*in a peremptory tone*) is everyone here? Let me see: Order to close and file away record of judicial inquiry, issued by the Milan tribunal . . . Aha, there's also the inquiry on that Rome anarchist group, headed by the dancer. Good! (*He stuffs documents into his briefcase, takes a dark overcoat and black hat off a coatrack and puts them on. At this point the inspector enters. Not recognizing the FOOL in this get-up, he is momentarily perplexed.*)

INSPECTOR. Good morning, what can I do for you? Were you looking for someone?

FOOL. No, Inspector, I came back to pick up my papers . . .

INSPECTOR. Oh, no, you again? Get out!

FOOL. Listen, maybe you're worried about your own problems; is that any reason to let it out on me?

INSPECTOR. Out! (*He half pushes, half pulls him to the door.*)

FOOL. For heaven's sake! Are you all neurotic in here? Starting with that crazy delinquent who's going around looking for you so he can bust you in the mouth.

INSPECTOR. (*stops for a moment*) Who's going around looking for me?

FOOL. Some guy, *dolce vita* type, in a turtleneck sweater; didn't he beat you up yet?

INSPECTOR. "Listen, that's enough; you've already wasted too much of my time. Do me a favor; get out of here! Scram!

FOOL. Forever? (*throws little farewell kisses, threatening gesture of anger from the INSPECTOR*) All right, all right, I'm going. Anyway, if you want a piece of advice, just because I think you're a nice guy . . . the minute you run into your "dolce vita" neighbor, duck! Take it from me. (*Exits; the INSPECTOR heaves a great sigh, then goes directly to the coatrack, which he finds completely empty.*)

INSPECTOR. (*running after the FOOL*) That sonofabitch! Pretending to be crazy so he can rip off people's coats! Hey, you! (*Bumps squarely into the POLICE-MAN, who is just coming in at this moment*) Chase after that nut, the one who was in here before. He's walking out with my coat and hat . . . maybe even the brief-case. Sure, that's mine too! Quick, before he gives us the slip.

POLICEMAN. Right away. Inspector. (*He stops just beyond the door, talking to someone on the outside, in the wings.*) Yes sir, the Inspector is here. Please come in.

(*turns to the INSPECTOR, who is shuffling through papers, looking for the sheets that were torn up by the FOOL*)

INSPECTOR. What the hell happened to those indictments? . . .

POLICEMAN. Mr. Bertozzo, the investigator from the political division is here; he would like to talk to you.

(*INSPECTOR BERTOZZO raises his head from the desk, gets up, and goes to meet his visitor, toward the wings right.*)

INSPECTOR. Hey, old buddy . . . I was just talking about you a minute ago with this crazy nut who was telling me—ha, ha, get this—as soon as you ran into me, you were going to give me—(*An arm shoots out from the wings. BERTOZZO finds himself literally flat on the ground, and just has the strength to finish his sentence*)—a sock in the mouth! (*collapses.*)

(*The FOOL's head appears in the doorway. He shouts.*)

FOOL. I *told* him to duck!

(*Lights out. In the darkness, a musical interlude; probably a grotesque sounding march, such as the kind used in vaudeville shows, long enough to allow time for a change of scene.*)

## SCENE 2

*Scene moves to the fourth floor. If possible, the scenery outside the office window should be rolled upwards so it looks like the office is moving up. The office here is much the same as the one in the first scene, except that the furniture is arranged differently. A large portrait of the president hangs on the wall. FOOL stands onstage, stock still, facing the window, his back to the entrance. After his first lines, the CAPTAIN enters.*

FOOL. Guilty. Guilty. Guilty.

CAPTAIN. (*in an undertone, to the POLICEMAN who is standing motionless by the door*) Who is that? What does he want?

OFFICER. I don't know, sir. He busted in here like he owned the place, just as if he was the big boss. He says he wants to talk to you and the chief.

CAPTAIN. (*who has been massaging his right hand continually*) Ah, he wants to talk to us? (*He approaches the FOOL in a rather obsequious manner*) Good afternoon, can I help you? I understand you were looking for me.

FOOL. (*gazes at him impassively, making the merest gesture of tipping his hat*) Good afternoon. (*His gaze rests on the hand which the inspector is still massaging.*) What happened to your hand?

CAPTAIN. Oh, nothing. May I ask who you are?

FOOL. You didn't hurt your hand? Then how come you're massaging it? Just like that, to make an interesting impression? Some sort of nervous tic?

CAPTAIN. (*shows signs of becoming annoyed*) Maybe. I asked you, would you care to explain who you are?!

FOOL. I used to know a bishop who massaged his hand like that . . . a Jesuit.

CAPTAIN. Am I mistaken, or are you—

FOOL. (*not paying the slightest attention*) You ought to see an analyst. That continuous massaging is a symptom of insecurity . . . also of a guilt complex, and sexual frustration. Do you have trouble with women, by any chance?

CAPTAIN. (*flying off the handle*) Oh, for Christ's sake! (*slams his fist on the table*)

FOOL. (*indicating the gesture*) Impulsive! That proves it, you see? Tell the truth: it's not a nervous tic . . . you punched somebody no more than fifteen minutes ago, admit it!

CAPTAIN. What do you mean, admit it? Instead of that, why don't you tell me, once and for all, who it is I have the honor of talking to . . . and you could also do me the favor of taking off your hat . . . while you're at it!

FOOL. You're right (*removes his hat with studied slowness*) But I wasn't keeping it on out of rudeness, believe me. It's just because of that open window. I can't stand drafts, especially on my head. Don't you have that problem? Look, do you suppose you could close it?

CAPTAIN. (*brusquely*) No, I can't.

FOOL. No matter, I am Dr. Antonio A. Antonio, first counsel of the High Court.

CAPTAIN. A judge? Oh Christ! (*He almost faints.*)

FOOL. Please don't call me that – you'll only confuse me. Yes, that's right, the former professor from the University of Rome. Small p in "professor," and with a comma between "the former" and "from," as usual.

CAPTAIN. (*befuddled*) I get it now. . . .

FOOL. (*aggressively ironic*) What do you get?

CAPTAIN. Nothing, nothing.

FOOL. Exactly. (*again aggressive*) That is: nothing at all! Who informed you that I was coming to check up officially on the investigation and the order to have it closed?

CAPTAIN. (*now on the ropes*) Well, actually . . . I . . .

FOOL. You'd better not lie. That's something that makes me horribly nervous. I have a nervous tic too; it hits me here, on my neck, the minute somebody tells me a fib. Look how it's trembling . . . look! Now, did you know about my arrival, or not?

CAPTAIN. (*swallowing nervously*) Yes, I knew . . . but I wasn't expecting it so soon . . . that's all.

FOOL. Right, and that's exactly why the superior council decided to do it early. We have our informers, too—so we caught you off-balance! hope you don't mind?

CAPTAIN. (*on more comfortable ground now*) No, not at all. (*The FOOL points to his trembling neck.*) I mean, yes . . . a good deal. (*gestures toward a chair*) But please sit down, and let me take your hat (*grabs it, then changes his mind*)—or perhaps you'd rather keep it on . . . ?

FOOL. Good heavens, no; you keep it if you like . . . it's not even mine, anyhow.

CAPTAIN. What? (*He goes toward the window.*) Would you like to have the window closed?

FOOL. Not at all, don't bother. But I would appreciate it if you'd call the Chief. We should get started as soon as possible.

CAPTAIN. Certainly. But wouldn't it be better to go over to his office? It's more comfortable.

FOOL. Yes . . . But that nasty business with the anarchist took place right here in this office, didn't it?

CAPTAIN. Yes, it was here . . .

FOOL. (*opening his arms wide*) Well, then! (*He sits down and takes some papers out of his briefcase. We then discover that he has another briefcase with him as well: a huge one, from which he removes a quantity of miscellaneous items: a magnifying glass, pair of tweezers, stapler, judge's wooden mallet, and finally a bound copy of the Criminal Code. Meanwhile, by the door, the INSPECTOR is murmuring something into the POLICEMAN'S ear. Continuing to organize his papers:*) I would prefer, Captain, that in my presence you always speak in a normal tone of voice!

CAPTAIN. Of course, I'm sorry. (*turning to the officer*) Ask the Chief to come over here right away, if he can.

FOOL. Even if he can't!

CAPTAIN. (*slavishly correcting himself*) Yes, even if he can't.

OFFICER. (*exiting*) Yes sir. (*looks for a moment at the judge, who is putting his documents in order. He has attached a number of them with thumbtacks to the side wall, the window frame and cabinet. All at once the CAPTAIN remembers something.*) Oh, that's right, the transcripts! (*He grabs the telephone and dials a number.*) Hello, may I please speak to Inspector Bertozzo? Where has he gone? To the Chief's office? (*He hangs up, then starts to dial another number. The FOOL interrupts him.*)

FOOL. Excuse me, Captain, if you don't mind . . .

CAPTAIN. Yes, your honor?

FOOL. This Inspector Bertozzo you're concerned with, does he have anything to do with the review of the investigation?

CAPTAIN. Yes, Well, I mean . . . since he has the file with all the documents in it —

FOOL. Oh, but that won't be necessary. I have everything here with me; why bother getting another copy? What's the point?

CAPTAIN. You're right, there's no point.

(*From outside we hear the approaching, angry voice of the POLICE CHIEF, who enters like a catapult. The officer follows close behind him, abashed and nervous.*)

POLICE CHIEF. I would like to know, Inspector, just what is this nonsense about me having to run over to your office even if I can't?

CAPTAIN. No, sir, you're right . . . that is, but since —

CHIEF. But since, my ass! Have you been promoted to my superior all of a sudden? I'll tell you right now, this high-handed attitude of yours doesn't please me one bit. Especially the way you've been treating your associates. To go around actually punching them in the face: for god's sake!

CAPTAIN. Ah, yes, but you see, Chief — Bertozzo didn't tell you about the razzberry, and that crack about the sub-basement in Calabria — (*The FOOL, pretending to put away his legal folders, is squatting behind the desk, hidden from view and immediately comes into view.*)

CHIEF. What the hell are you talking about, razzberry! Come on, quit acting like a kid. We should be laying low, instead, with everybody watching us . . . and those goddam reporters talking about . . . spreading a bunch of lousy rumors . . . and quit trying to shut me up! I can say anything I — (*The INSPECTOR points to the false judge, who pretends to take no notice of the proceedings.*) Oh my god, who is that — a reporter? Why didn't you tell me —

FOOL. (*without looking up from his papers*) Don't

worry, Chief, I'm not a reporter. There won't be any kinds of rumors, I assure you.

CHIEF. I appreciate it.

FOOL. I understand and share your concern; in fact, I tried scolding your young associate here, even before you did.

CHIEF. (*turning to the CAPTAIN*) Really?

FOOL. I noticed that this young man has a rather irritable and intolerant character; now it appears, from your conversation, that he's also allergic to the razzberry — Do you know anything about the subject? (*He draws him aside in a confidential manner, while the CHIEF follows him with astonishment.*)

CHIEF. No, I really . . .

FOOL. (*speaking almost into his ear*) Take my advice, Chief; I'm talking to you like a father: this boy needs a good psychiatrist. Here, send him to this friend of mine; he's a genius. (*hands him a card*) Dr. Antonio A. Antonio, the former professor . . . but don't overlook the comma.

CHIEF. (*not knowing how to extricate himself*) Thanks very much, but if you don't mind, I —

FOOL. (*suddenly changing tone*) But of course I don't mind, of course. Please sit down and let's begin . . . By the way, did your associate inform you that I —

CAPTAIN. No, I'm sorry but I didn't have time. (*turning to the CHIEF*) Dr. Antonio A. Antonio, he is first counsellor of the High Court . . .

FOOL. For heaven's sake, forget about that "first counsellor;" it doesn't mean a thing to me . . . why not just say "one of the first," and let it go at that!

CAPTAIN. If you prefer.

CHIEF. (*having great difficulty in recovering from the blow*) Your honor . . . I really had no . . .

CAPTAIN. (*coming to his aid*) The judge is here to conduct a review of the investigation about the case—

CHIEF. (*with an unexpected impulse*) Ah, certainly, certainly, we were expecting you!

FOOL. (*to the INSPECTOR*) You see? Your Chief is much more honest! He puts his cards right on the table! You should follow his example! But of course, this is another generation, a different breed . . .

CHIEF. Yes, a different breed.

FOOL. Listen, I hope you don't mind my telling you this now, but you seem — how can I say it — almost familiar to me . . . as if I had met you somewhere, many years ago. In a concentration camp, perhaps?

CHIEF. (*stammering*) A concentration camp?

FOOL. Oh, what am I saying? You, director of a concentration camp? Ridiculous idea . . . (*staring at CHIEF, who literally collapses into a chair and nervously lights a cigarette*) Now then, let's get down to the transcript. (*leafs through some papers*) On the evening of — the date doesn't matter — an anarchist, railway signalman by profession, was brought to this room for questioning on his alleged participation in the dynamiting of a bank, which caused the death of sixteen innocent citizens. Now, this is an exact quotation from you, Chief: "There was serious circumstantial evidence against him." Did you say that?

CHIEF. Yes, your honor, at the beginning. Later on —

FOOL. That's just where we are, at the beginning. Let's proceed in order: toward midnight, the anarchist, seized by a fit of *raptus* — it's still you, Chief, who are talking — seized by *raptus*, threw himself out of the window, crashing to the ground. Now, what is "raptus?" Bandieu states that "raptus" is an exasperated form of suicidal anguish which seizes even psychologically healthy individuals, if they are provoked to violent anxiety; to desperate suffering. Correct?

CHIEF AND CAPTAIN. Correct.

FOOL. Then we have to find out who or what caused this anxiety, this anguish. We have no choice but to reconstruct the events of that day. Chief, your entrance, please.

CHIEF. My entrance?

FOOL. Yes, yours. And with feeling, please.

CHIEF. What entrance, your honor?

FOOL. The one that caused the raptus.

CHIEF. Your honor, I think there's been a mistake. It was not *my* entrance but an assistant of mine . . .

FOOL. Eh, eh, it's not nice to throw the responsibility onto your own staff members; in fact, it's rather naughty. Come on, get yourself together and play your part . . .

CAPTAIN. But judge, it was one of those expedients that's often used, in every police department . . . just a normal procedure to make the suspect confess.

FOOL. I don't recall asking for your opinion! Please be good enough to let your superior officer speak! You're very rude, you know that? From now on, answer only when spoken to, understand? Now, Chief, please play that entrance scene for me, in first person. Go ahead, and give it all you've got.

CHIEF. All right. (*He starts to go to the door.*) It went something like this. The suspected anarchist was sitting there — where you are now. The inspector . . . I mean, I . . . sort of burst in . . . (*He bursts in.*)

FOOL. Beautiful. Beautiful.

CHIEF. And . . . and I layed into him.

FOOL. Come on, be specific. Give me detail. I want to be able to know what you're thinking. I want to be able to know what you had for breakfast.

CHIEF. "Okay, my railroad worker friend . . . you subversive . . . you better fess up."

FOOL. ( *with file on his lap, his glasses now on top of his head*) No! No! Keep to the script! ( *waves the script*) That's not what you say!

CHIEF. Oh right. Okay. I say: "You've messed around long enough."

FOOL. ( *looking at the files*) "Messed around." Is that all you say?

CHIEF. Yes, I swear to God.

FOOL. I believe you. Keep going. Finish him off.

CHIEF. "We have proof that you were the one who planted the bombs in the station."

FOOL. What bombs?

CHIEF. ( *in a more conversational tone*) I'm talking about the terrorist attack that happened on the twenty-fifth of—

FOOL. No, answer with the same words you used that evening. Pretend I'm the anarchist railroad man. Come on, don't be afraid: what bombs?

CHIEF. Don't give me that innocent act! You know exactly what bombs I'm talking about: the ones you people planted in the railway cars at the central station, eight months ago.

FOOL. But did you really have the proof?

CHIEF. No, but just like the Captain was trying to explain before, it was one of the usual tricks we police officers apply pretty often.

FOOL. Ha, Ha! What a line! ( *He whaps the dumbfounded CHIEF on the shoulder.*)

CHIEF. But we did have suspicions . . . Seeing as how the suspect was the only anarchist railroad worker in Milan, it was easy to deduce that he was the one . . .

FOOL. Of course, of course; I would say it's obvious,

self-evident. So, if it's beyond doubt that a railroad worker planted the bombs in the railway, we can also logically deduce that it was a judge who planted those famous bombs in the Rome courthouse, the commander of the guard put the ones under the monument to the unknown soldier, and that the bomb in the Agricultural Bank was left either by a banker or by a farmer, take your choice.[11] (*flying into a sudden rage*) Come on, gentlemen, I'm here to carry out a serious examination, not to play idiotic logical games! Let's continue! It says here (*He reads from a page.*) "The anarchist did not seem affected by the accusation, but smiled in disbelief." Who made this statement?

CAPTAIN. I did, your honor.

FOOL. Good, so he was smiling . . . But there's another remark here, in your own precise words — which were also repeated by the judge who closed the investigation: "fear of losing his position, of being fired, definitely contributed to the suspect's suicidal breakdown." So, one minute he's smiling and the next he's a desperate man. Who told him he was going to be fired?

CAPTAIN. It wasn't me — I swear to . . .

FOOL. Now now fellas — this is reality I'm talking about. Reality, with warts, and dirty hair and heavy breathing, like in the movies. You guys want to come off looking like a bunch of puffs? Every policeman in the world's got to come down hard sometime, it's expected. But you stand here claiming you never took off the kid gloves. I mean, it's your right to use force.

CHIEF AND CAPTAIN. Thank you, your honor.

FOOL. You're welcome. On the other hand, as we know, it can be risky sometimes — you tell an anarchist: "things don't look so hot for you; when we tell the railroad managers you're an anarchist, they'll throw you out in the street — canned!'' And he gets depressed . . . The truth is that an anarchist cares about his job more than anything else. Basically, they're petty-bourgeois . . . attached to their small comforts: fixed salary every month, benefits, bonus, retirement pension, health insurance, a tranquil old age . . . believe me, nobody thinks about his own retirement more than an anarchist. Of course, I'm talking about our own home-grown variety, those easygoing, domesticated types. Nothing like the ones we used to have back in the old days! Those were always being hounded from one country to another. You know something about that, Chief — people being hounded? Oh goodness, what am I saying?! Well, then, to recapitulate: you beat the anarchist down emotionally, he becomes angry and depressed, and throws himself out —

CAPTAIN. If you'll allow me, your honor — in all honesty, it didn't happen right away. You haven't gotten to my part yet.

FOOL. You're right, so I haven't. The first part happened while you were still out, Inspector. Then you came back in, and after a dramatic pause he said — come on, Inspector, recite your line, still making believe that I'm the anarchist.

CAPTAIN. All right, of course: ''they just called me from Rome. There's some good news for you — '' Excuse me, can I try that again?

FOOL. Of course, and take your time.

CAPTAIN. (*nods, goes out, enters, pause*) ''They just called me from Milan. There's some good news for you: your comrade has confessed to planting the bomb in that bank in Milan.''

FOOL. And the railroad worker, how did he take it? What should I do?

CAPTAIN. He turned pale, and asked for a cigarette.

FOOL. "Could I have a cigarette?" And then as you reached to get one—he jumps out of the window!

CAPTAIN. No, not yet.

FOOL. But that's what it says here.

CHIEF. Let me see that. (*looks at file*) You have the first draft, your honor. (*more torn pages*) We did some rewrites. Here.

FOOL. Oh, I'm sorry.

CHIEF. Don't worry about it.

FOOL. (*looking through the file*) I see that you told members of the press that before his tragic gesture, the anarchist felt trapped. He was "cornered." Did you say that?

CHIEF. Yes, that's just what I said: "cornered."

FOOL. And then what else did you say?

CHIEF. That his alibi, his story about spending the famous afternoon of the terrorist attack playing cards in a bar down by the canal, had collapsed. It didn't hold up anymore.

FOOL. Therefore, that the anarchist was under heavy suspicion for the Milan bank bombings, as well as for the attacks against the trains. And in conclusion, you added that the anarchist's suicidal act was "an obvious gesture of self-accusation."

CHIEF. Yes, I said so.

FOOL. And you, Inspector, shouted that during his life the man had been a delinquent, a troublemaker. But after only a few weeks, you, Chief, declared—here's the document—that "naturally," I repeat "naturally," there was no concrete evidence against the poor guy. Correct? Therefore, he was entirely innocent. You yourself even commented, Captain, "that anarchist was a good kid."

CHIEF. Yes, I'll admit . . . we made a mistake . . .

FOOL. Good grief, anybody can make a mistake. But you boys, if you'll pardon my saying so, really laid a big one. First of all you arbitrarily detain a free citizen, then abuse your authority by keeping him over the legal time limit, after which you traumatize the poor signalman by telling him you've got proof that he set the dynamite in the railway; then you more or less deliberately give him the psychosis that he's going to lose his job, then that his alibi about the card game has collapsed; and finally, the last straw: that his friend and comrade from Rome has confessed to being guilty of the Milan massacre — his friend is a dirty killer!? To the point that he cries out in desperation, "this is the end of the anarchist movement," and jumps out! My god, are we all crazy? By this time, who could be surprised if somebody who's been worked over like that gets a fit of "raptus"?! Oh, no, no, no; I'm sorry, but in my opinion you are guilty, and how! You're totally responsible for the anarchists's death! With grounds for immediate indictment on charges of inciting to suicide!

CHIEF. But your honor, how can it be possible?! You admitted yourself that it's our job to interrogate suspects, and in order to get them to talk, every once in a while we have use tricks, traps, occasional psychological violence —

FOOL. Oh no, in this case we're not talking about "occasional," but about continuous violence! First of all, just to raise one example: did you have absolute proof that that poor railroad man lied about his own alibi, yes or no? Answer me!

CHIEF. No, we didn't have any absolute proof . . . but —

FOOL. I'm not interested in your "buts!" Are there two

or three pensioners who still back up his alibi, yes or no?

CAPTAIN. Yes, there are.

FOOL. So, you also lied to the press and TV when you said the alibi had collapsed and there were serious motives for suspicion? Then you don't use those traps, schemes, lies and so on just to trip up suspects, but also to take advantage of those gullible assholes out there — to astound their good faith! All right, then, Inspector, you answer me this time: where did you get the news that the anarchist dancer had confessed?

CAPTAIN. We made it up ourselves.

FOOL. Wow, what imagination! You two ought to be writers. And believe me, you may get the chance. Jail is a great place for writing. Depressed, eh? Well then, to be perfectly honest, I'd better let you know that they have overwhelming proof of extremely serious counts against you in Rome. You're both washed up! The department of Justice and department of the Interior have decided to get rid of you, to make the worst possible example out of you, in order to build up the credibility of the police — since practically nobody believes in them anymore!

CHIEF. No, it's impossible!

CAPTAIN. But how could they — ?

FOOL. Sure, two careers ruined. That's politics, my friends. First you came in handy for a certain scheme: union agitation had to be put down; there was a real witch-hunting climate. But now things have turned around a little . . . people are up in arms about the death of that defenestrated anarchist; they're demanding a couple of heads, and the state is going to give them what they want!

CHIEF. *Our* heads?!

CAPTAIN. Exactly!

FOOL. There's an old English proverb that says: "the

nobleman sets his hounds against the peasants, and if the peasants complain to the king, the nobleman seeks pardon by killing the hounds."

CHIEF. And you think . . . really . . . you're certain?

FOOL. Why do you suppose I'm here? It's my job to deliver judgement on you.

CAPTAIN. Damned job!

CHIEF. I know who stabbed me in the back. Ah, but I'll get even with him!

FOOL. Of course, there are a lot of people who'll gloat over your misfortune . . . snicker with satisfaction . . .

CAPTAIN. Sure, beginning with our colleagues. That's the thing that really makes me see red!

CHIEF. Not to mention the press.

CAPTAIN. They'll drag us through the mud. Can't you just see the daily scandal sheets?!

CHIEF. You can imagine what kind of stuff they'll say about us — those bastards, who used to come around licking our hands . . . they'll turn into a regular lynch mob!

CAPTAIN. "He was a sadist." "He was an animal."

FOOL. And don't forget the humiliation . . . the ironic laughter . . .

CHIEF. The snide remarks . . . everybody will be turning their backs — we won't even be able to get jobs as parking lot attendants!

CAPTAIN. Lousy goddam world!

FOOL. No, lousy goddam government!

CHIEF. At this point, maybe you can tell us — is there anything left for us to do? Please give us some advice!

FOOL. Me? What can I tell you?

CAPTAIN. Yes, advise us!

FOOL. If I were in your shoes . . .

CHIEF. In our shoes?

FOOL. I would throw myself out the window!

CHIEF AND CAPTAIN. What?

FOOL. You asked for my advice. And under the circumstances, rather than put up with that kind of humiliation . . . jump! Go on, you can do it!

CHIEF. Yes, O.K., but how will that change anything?!

FOOL. Exactly, it won't change anything. Just give in to the "raptus" and jump! (*He pushes them both toward the window.*)

CAPTAIN AND CHIEF. No, don't! Wait!

FOOL. What do you mean, "wait?" What is there to wait for? What's the point of staying in this filthy world? You call this a life? Lousy world, lousy government . . . Lousy everything! Let's jump out! (*drags them forward with such violence that he nearly rips their clothes*)

CHIEF. No, please, your honor, what are you doing? I've still got hope!

FOOL. There's no more hope. You're both finished, can't you understand that? Finished! Out!!

CHIEF AND CAPTAIN. Help! Don't push . . . please! No!

FOOL. I'm not the one who's pushing; it's the "raptus." Horray for liberating "raptus!" (*He grabs them by the belt and forces them up onto the window ledge.*)

CHIEF AND CAPTAIN. No, no! help! help!! (*The PO-LICE OFFICER, who had left the room at the beginning of the interrogation, comes back in.*)

OFFICER. What's going on, sir?

FOOL. (*relaxing his grip*) Oh, nothing, nothing happened. Right, Inspector? Right, Chief? Go ahead, put your officer's mind at ease.

CHIEF. (*visibly shaken, climbing down from the ledge*) Oh, sure, relax . . . it was only—

FOOL. A "raptus."

OFFICER. A "raptus?"

FOOL. Yes, they tried to throw themselves out of the window.

OFFICER. Them too?

FOOL. Yes, but for heaven's sake, don't tell the reporters!

OFFICER. No, no.

CAPTAIN. But it's not true; it was you, judge, who tried—

CHIEF. right!

OFFICER. You tried to jump out, your honor?

CHIEF. No, he was pushing.

FOOL. It's true, it's true: I was pushing them. And they almost went along with it; they were desperate. The smallest pretext is sufficient when one is desperate . . .

OFFICER. Yeah, gee, the smallest pretext.

FOOL. And look at them, they're still desperate. Look what long faces!

OFFICER. (*inspired by the judge's confidence*) Yeah, they sure do look . . . excuse the expression . . . a little up shit creek, as they say—

CHIEF. Hey, have you gone out of your mind?

OFFICER. I'm sorry, I meant in the hole.

FOOL. Come on, cheer up—and flush it all down, as they say. Sunny side up, gentlemen!

CHIEF. Sure, it's easy for you to talk. In our position —I swear to you, for a minute there I was almost ready to jump for real!

OFFICER. You were about to jump? In person?

CAPTAIN. So was I, in fact.

FOOL. There, gentlemen, you see. When they use the term "raptus?!" And who would have been at fault?

CHIEF. Those bastards in the government, who else!? First they push you: "come down hard; create a climate of subversion, of threatened social disorder" . . .

CAPTAIN. ". . . of the need for an authoritarian state!" You throw yourself into the job, and the next thing you know—.

FOOL. No, not at all. The fault would have been entirely my own.

CHIEF. Yours? Why?

FOOL. Because none of it is true; I invented the whole thing.

CHIEF. What do you mean? Isn't it true that they want to get rid of us in Rome?

FOOL. No, that's the last thing on their minds.

CAPTAIN. And the overwhelming proof?

FOOL. There never was any proof.

CAPTAIN. And the story about the cabinet minister who wanted our heads?

FOOL. All hogwash. The cabinet ministers are crazy about you; you're the apple of their eye. And the head police commissioner gets all mushy and sentimental every time he hears your name—and calls his mother!

CHIEF. You're not joking, are you?

FOOL. Absolutely not! The whole government loves you! And I'll tell you another thing: the English proverb about the nobleman killing his hounds is false, too. No lord ever killed a good hunting dog to satisfy a peasant! If anything, it's been the other way around. And if the hound gets killed in the free-for-all, the King immediately sends a sympathy telegram to the nobleman. Along with flowers and funeral wreaths! (*The CAPTAIN pre-*

*pares to say something, but the CHIEF nervously stops him.*)

CAPTAIN. If I didn't misunderstand you.

CHIEF. Of course you misunderstood. Let me talk, Inspector.

CAPTAIN. Yes sir, excuse me.

CHIEF. I don't understand, your honor, why you wanted to invent this tall story—

FOOL. Tall story? No, it's just one of those normal "exaggerations" or "tricks" which the high court also uses sometimes, to show the police how uncivilized such methods are—not to say criminal!

CHIEF. Then you're still convinced that if the anarchist threw himself out of the window, we were the ones to urge him on?

FOOL. You proved it to me yourselves a moment ago, when you lost control!

CAPTAIN. But we weren't present at the moment when he jumped. Ask the officer!

OFFICER. Yes, your honor, they had just left the room when he jumped out!

FOOL. That's like saying that if someone sets a bomb inside a bank and then leaves, he's not guilty, because he wasn't there at the time of the explosion!! Oh, we're really on the ball with our logic around here!

CHIEF. No, no, your honor; there's been a misunderstanding . . . the officer was referring to the first version. We're talking about the second one.

FOOL. Ah, that's right . . . because at a later stage, there was a sort of retraction.

CHIEF. Well, I wouldn't say exactly a retraction. A simple correction . . .

FOOL. Right. Let's hear it: what did you correct? (*The CHIEF nods to the CAPTAIN.*)

CAPTAIN. Well, we—

FOOL. I warn you that I also have the transcripts of this new version. Please continue.

CAPTAIN. We corrected the time of the . . . what should I call it . . . of the trick.

FOOL. What do you mean by the time of the trick?

CHIEF. Yes, to make a long story short, we stated that we set the trap for the anarchist, telling him those stories and whatnot, around eight o'clock in the evening instead of at midnight.

CAPTAIN. At twenty hundred hours, in other words.

FOOL. Ah, you set everything, including the flight from the window, at four hours earlier! A kind of super-extended daylight savings time!

CAPTAIN. No, not the flight—that still happened at midnight, with no change. There were witnesses.

CHIEF. One of them was that reporter who was standing down there in the courtyard, remember? (*The judge shakes his head no.*) The one who heard the thumping noises on the building ledge and then on the ground, and was the first to come running . . . he made a note of the time right away.

FOOL. All right. The suicide took place at midnight and the fairytale session at eight. So where do we stand with the raptus? After all, barring contrary evidence, your entire version of the suicide is based on that raptus. Every one of you, from the examining judge to the district attorney, has always insisted on the fact that the poor slob threw himself out, "the cause being *sudden* raptus" . . . and now, right at the best part, you're dumping the "raptus."

CHIEF. No, no—we're not dumping the "raptus" at all—

FOOL. You are too dumping it!: you're moving the

suicide a full four hours up from the moment when you, or that associate of yours, come in and play the big "proof, proof, we've got the proof" game with him. And where does that leave the "sudden raptus?" After four hours, you've got to be kidding; the anarchist would have had time to digest an even bigger slice of baloney than the one you fed him. You could have told him Bakunin was a fink working as an informer for the police and the Vatican: it would have been the same!

CHIEF. But that was exactly what we wanted, your honor!

FOOL. You wanted to tell him Bakunin was a fink?

CHIEF. No, we wanted to prove that the "raptus" couldn't have been caused by our deceptions, by our false statements . . . in other words, precisely because four hours passed between that time and moment of the suicide!

FOOL. Why yes, of course, you're right. What a first-rate idea . . . you really are sharp!

CHIEF. Thanks, your honor.

FOOL. Of course; it's certain that this way nobody can lay the blame on you: there was a nasty fib, but it can't be considered a determining factor!

CAPTAIN. Exactly. Therefore we're innocent.

FOOL. Good for you, boys. Of course, now it's not clear why that poor jerk threw himself out the window. But that's not important; for now the important thing is that you come out innocent.

CHIEF. Thanks again. I'll tell you sincerely, I was afraid that you started out with your mind already made up about us.

FOOL. Already made up?

CAPTAIN. Yes, that you wanted us guilty at any cost.

FOOL. For goodness' sake. If anything, it's just the

opposite: I'll tell you, if I acted a little harsh and aggressive, it was only so that you'd be forced to come up with the kind of evidence and arguments that would allow me to help you as much as possible to come out on top.

CHIEF. I'm sincerely touched. It's wonderful to know that the High Court is still the police department's best friend!

FOOL. Let's say collaborator.

CAPTAIN AND CHIEF. Yes, let's call it that.

FOOL. But you have to collaborate, too, so that I can help you all the way . . . and place you in an unassailable position.

CHIEF. Of course.

CAPTAIN. We'd be delighted.

FOOL. First of all, we have to provide irrefutable arguments proving that during those four hours the anarchist had entirely gotten over his depression — his famous psychological breakdown, as the judge who closed the investigation referred to it.

CAPTAIN. Well, there's the testimony of the officer here, and mine too, stating that the anarchist felt better after a first, brief period of distress . . .

FOOL. Is it in the transcript?

CAPTAIN. Yes, I think so.

FOOL. Yes, yes, it is there; it's included in the second version of the facts. Here it is (*reads*) "the railroad worker calmed down and stated that he and the ex-dancer were not on good terms." Excellent!

FOOL. And let's not forget that our friend the railroad worker was aware of the fact that loads of spies and police informers hung around the anarchist group in Rome. He had even said so to the dancer: "the police and fascists are using you to foment unrest . . . you're swarming with paid provocateurs, who push you in any direction they want. And the entire left is going to pay the price for it."

CAPTAIN. Maybe that's exactly why they had the fight!

FOOL. Right, and since the dancer didn't listen to him, maybe our railroad worker was beginning to suspect that he was a provocateur himself.

CHIEF. Ah, could be.

FOOL. Therefore, since he didn't give a damn about him, there's your irrefutable proof: the anarchist was calm.

CAPTAIN. In fact, he was actually smiling. Remember, I said so myself, back in the first version.

FOOL. Yes, but unfortunately there's the problem that in the first version you also stated that the anarchist, looking "beaten-down," had lit a cigarette and commented in a tragic voice, "this is the end of the anarchist movement." Dum da-dum dum! Now what ever gave you the bright idea of putting in that kind of melodramatic note—for crying out loud!

CHIEF. You're right, your honor. The fact is that it was this young man's idea. I even told him, look, let's leave the big dramatic scenes to movie directors—we're cops!

FOOL. Listen to me: at this point, if we want to find a coherent solution, the only way to figure out what's going on is to throw everything up in the air and start all over again from the beginning.

CAPTAIN. Should we construct a third version?

FOOL. Good God, no! All we have to do is lend more plausibility to the two we already have.

CHIEF. Right.

FOOL. All right then, point one, first rule: what's been said is said, and there's no more turning back. Therefore it's established that you, Captain, and you, Chief—or someone operating under your orders—told the fairy-tales; that the anarchist smoked his last cigarette and recited his melodramatic line . . . but, and this is where the variant comes in, he did not throw himself out the window, because it wasn't yet midnight but only eight o'clock.

CHIEF. As in the second version.

FOOL. And, as we know, a railroad worker always follows the timetable.

CHIEF. The fact is that this way we have all the time we need to make him change his mood . . . enough so that we could have him delay his suicidal impulse.

CAPTAIN. It's a flawless argument!

FOOL. True, but how did this change come about? Time alone isn't enough to heal certain wounds. Somebody must have helped him. I don't know, through a few gestures or—

OFFICER. I gave him a piece of chewing gum!

FOOL. Good. And what about you two?

CHIEF. Well, I wasn't there . . .

FOOL. Oh, no, this is too delicate a moment, you had to be there!

CHIEF. O.K., I was there.

FOOL. All right, so to begin with, can we say that the worried state of mind which had taken hold of the anarchist made you feel a bit sorry for him?

CAPTAIN. Yes, I really did feel sorry for him.

FOOL. And could we add that you were sorry for having made him feel so bitter and depressed—right, Chief? You being such a sensitive man!

CHIEF. Well, yes, basically I found him rather pathetic. I was sorry.

FOOL. Perfect! And I bet you couldn't help putting a hand on his shoulder.

CHIEF. No, I don't think so.

FOOL. Oh, come on, it's a paternal gesture.

CHIEF. Well, maybe, but I don't remember.

FOOL. I'm sure you did! Please, tell me you did!

OFFICER. Yes, that's right, he did—I saw him!

CHIEF. Well, if he saw me . . .

FOOL. (*turning to the CAPTAIN*) And you gave him a friendly smack on the cheek, like this. (*smacks him*)

CAPTAIN. No, I'm sorry to disappoint you, but I'm positive I didn't . . . I didn't give him any smacks.

FOOL. You certainly do disappoint me. And you know why? Because, in addition to being an anarchist, that man was also a railroad worker! Had you forgotten? And you know what being a railroad worker means? It means something that's tied to everyone's childhood. It means little electric and mechanical model trains. Didn't you have any model trains when you were a child?

CAPTAIN. Yes, I had a real steam engine, with smoke coming out . . . and armor-plated cars, naturally.

FOOL. And did it go "too-toot?"

CAPTAIN. Yes, too-toot . . .

FOOL. Splendid! You said "too-toot," and your eyes lit up! No, Captain, you couldn't help feeling affection for that man . . . because, subconsciously, he was connected to your little train. If the suspect had been, say, a bank clerk, you wouldn't have even looked at him. But he was a railroad man, and you, I'm more than certain, gave him a smack.

OFFICER. Yes, it's true; I saw it myself . . . he did give it to him: two smacks!

FOOL. You see? I have witnesses! And what did you say while you were smacking him?

CAPTAIN. I don't remember—

FOOL. *I'll* tell you what you said; you said to him:

"come on, chin up, don't take it so hard . . . (*and you called him by name*) you'll see, the anarchist movement won't die!"

CAPTAIN. Gee, I really don't think —

FOOL. Oh, no — by god, you said it. Otherwise I'll get mad. Look at this nerve on my neck. Do you admit you said it, yes or no?

CAPTAIN. Oh, all right, if it makes you happy.

FOOL. Well, then, say it. I have to put it down in the transcript. (*begins to write*)

CAPTAIN. Well, I said: come on, chin up . . . don't take it so hard, kid . . . you'll see, the anarchist movement won't die!

FOOL. Fine . . . and then you sang.

CHIEF. We sang . . . ?

FOOL. Naturally, once you got to that point . . . there was an atmosphere of such friendship, such comradeship, that you couldn't help singing — all together, in chorus! Let's hear what you sang. I bet it was the anarchist hymn, "The world is our homeland."

CHIEF. No, your honor; I'm sorry, but as far as singing in chorus is concerned we really can't go along —

FOOL. Ah, you don't go along? Well, then, you know what I say? I'll drop the whole thing, and you can work it out for yourselves. It's your problem. I'll arrange the facts exactly as you've laid them out for me: you know the outcome. It will be — excuse the colorful expression — a fucking mess! That's right! First you say one thing, then you retract it; you offer one version and half an hour later you offer a completely different one. You don't even agree between the two of you. You make statements to the entire press, and to TV news reporters too, if I'm not mistaken, of this nature: "naturally" there isn't any transcript of the interrogation sessions with the anarchist; there was no time—and then, after a while, a miracle!: two or three transcripts turn up . . . and signed by him, with his own hand, large as life! If any suspect contradicted himself half as much as you muckers, he'd have gotten bumped off long ago. You know what people think of you by now? That you're a bunch of bull-shitters . . . as well as bad boys. How can you expect anybody to believe what you say anymore? Except for the judge who ordered the inquiry to be closed, of course. And you know the main reason why people don't believe you? Because your version of the facts, in addition to being screwy, is also lacking in human interest . . . warmth. Nobody, Captain, can forget the rude, arrogant way you answered the anarchist's poor widow, when she asked you why she hadn't been notified of her husband's death. Never a moment of sympathy; not one of you who ever lets himself go . . . exposes himself . . . maybe laughs, cries—sings! People would be willing to forgive all the contradictions you've jumped into with both feet—but only if, in exchange, beyond these obstacles, they could catch a glimpse of a human heart . . . two "living" men who let themselves be moved to tears of sympathy; and although still remaining policemen, join the anarchist in singing his own song, just to make him happy . . . "Arise ye prisoners of starvation."—who wouldn't burst out crying!? Who could refuse to joyfully call out your names, on hearing such a story! I beg of you! For your own good . . . so that the investigation will turn out in your favor . . . Sing! (*He begins singing the* International *in English in a low voice, motioning to the policemen. Shakily, and with obvious embarrassment, they start singing along with him, one after the other.*)

"Arise yet prisoners of starvation
Arise ye wretched of the earth
For justice thunders condemnation
A better world's in birth."

(*He actually grabs them by the shoulders, urging them on. Lights begin to go on in houses outside the window, all around town, as policemen become a full-voiced chorus.*)

## END OF ACT ONE

# ACT TWO

*Even before the lights go on, the four men begin singing
again just as at the end of Act I. The resolute final
notes coincide with the return of full stage lighting.*

FOOL. (*applauds, embraces and shakes hands with the
policemen*) Wonderful, good for you! Now that's more
like it! At this point nobody can doubt that the anarchist
felt completely tranquil!

CAPTAIN. I would guess he was happy.

FOOL. Sure, he felt right at home. Among members of
one of those Roman clubs where in fact there are more
plainclothes police than real anarchists.

CHIEF. Our rapid-fire attack of false statements didn't
damage his psychological state in the least.

FOOL. Therefore, no raptus; the raptus comes later.
(*indicating the CAPTAIN*) When?

CAPTAIN. Towards midnight.

FOOL. Caused by what?

CHIEF. Well, I think the reason—

FOOL. No, no, good lord! You don't think anything;
you're not supposed to know anything about it, Chief!

CHIEF. What do you mean, I'm not supposed to
know—?

FOOL. For god's sake, here we are bending over back-
wards to get you out of the mess, to show that you had
nothing to do with the railroad man's death, because you
weren't even present . . .

CHIEF. I'm sorry, you're right. I was distracted.

FOOL. Eh, but you get a little too distracted, Chief. Pay
more attention! So, as a line from an old vaudeville rou-

54

tine goes, "headquarters had no head, 'cause the head man was in bed." But the Captain wasn't in bed!

CAPTAIN. No, I was in the office, but I went out a little while later.

FOOL. Here we go shifting responsibility again. Now, be a good boy and tell me what happened around midnight.

CAPTAIN. There were six of us in this room; myself, four officers . . . and a lieutenant.

FOOL. Ah, yes, the one they promoted to captain later on.

CAPTAIN. That's right.

FOOL. And what was going on?

CAPTAIN. The interrogation.

FOOL. Still? "Where were you; what were you doing? Talk! Don't try playing any smart tricks."

CAPTAIN. Oh, no, your honor. We were kidding around during the interrogation.

FOOL. Come on. "Kidding around?"

CAPTAIN. I swear to you . . . ask the guard. (*He shoves the OFFICER toward the judge.*)

FOOL. That isn't necessary. It's incredible (*exhibits a sheet of paper*) but it's even written down here in the deposition given before the judge who closed the inquiry.

CAPTAIN. Certainly, and he didn't question it in the least.

FOOL. Oh, I believe it too. But how do you mean, "kidding around?"

CAPTAIN. In the sense that we were kidding . . . we were interrogating him trying to get a laugh out of it.

FOOL. I don't understand; were you putting on a slapstick comedy? Did you wear clown suits and blow on tooters?

CAPTAIN. Well, we didn't exactly go that far . . . but

anyway we went heavy on the joking, playing around with the suspects . . . making puns, a couple of funny routines . . .

OFFICER. It's true, honest, we were laughing like crazy. The Captain may not look it, but, you know, he's a real comedian. When he's in the right mood, you should see the side-splitting interrogations he does . . . ha, ha, ha, you could die laughing!

FOOL. Now I understand why they decided to change your motto in Rome.

CHIEF. The motto of the police force?

FOOL. Yes, yours. They decided at the Ministry of the Interior.

CHIEF. Are they going to change it?

FOOL. Well, let's say they're going to complete it. How does it go now?

CAPTAIN. The police is at the service of the citizens.

FOOL. That's it; and from now on it will be "the police is at the service of the citizens, to entertain them!"

CHIEF. Ha, ha; you're making fun of us.

FOOL. Not at all; I'm more than convinced that you treat suspects jokingly, as you assert I recall once I was in Bergamo—during the interrogation of that so-called "Monday league"—remember, there was a priest involved in it; also a doctor, the druggist . . . almost a whole town indicted, and later turned out to be innocent. Anyway, I was living in a small hotel right near the police headquarters where the interrogations were taking place, and almost every night I was woken up by screaming and yelling which at first I thought came from people being kicked, clubbed . . . but later I found out it was laughter. Yes, rather coarse laughter from the people under interrogation: "Ah, ah, oh god! Enough, ah, ah! Help, I can't stand it! No more, Inspector; you're killing me!"

CHIEF. Irony notwithstanding, you know that afterward they got sentenced, from the commandant to the lowest corporal. All of them!

FOOL. Certainly, for overdoing the humor! (*expressions of impatience from the officers*) No, no, I'm not joking; you don't realize how many perfectly innocent people invent crimes just so they can be brought in to headquarters! You think they're anarchists, communists, militants in Workers' Power, union organizers . . . it's not true; actually they're nothing but poor, sick, depressed people; sad hypochondriacs masquerading as revolutionaries just so you can interrogate them! That's the only way they can finally achieve some good, healthy laughter—perk up their tired blood, in other words!

CHIEF. Right now, your honor, I would say that you're doing more than pulling our leg; you're actually mocking us!

FOOL. Good heavens, I would never allow it.

CHIEF. (*hunching and rubbing his shoulders*) Excuse me, would you mind if I closed the window? It's gotten so cold in here all of a sudden . . .

FOOL. Certainly, go right ahead. It really is cold!

CAPTAIN. That's because the sun has just gone down. (*At a sign from the CAPTAIN, the POLICEMAN has closed the window.*)

FOOL. Right. But then, on that evening, the sun didn't go down.

CAPTAIN. Huh?

FOOL. I said, on that evening when the anarchist threw himself out the window, did the sun stay up; wasn't there any sunset? (*The three policemen look at each other in astonishment.*)

CHIEF. I don't follow . . . (*The FOOL pretends to get annoyed.*)

FOOL. Look, even though it was December, if the window was still wide open at midnight, it means it wasn't cold. And if it wasn't cold, that could only have been because the sun hadn't gone down yet. It went down later: at one A.M., like in July in Norway.

CHIEF. No, no; they had just opened it . . . to air out the room, right?

CAPTAIN. Yes, it was full of smoke.

OFFICER. The anarchist smoked a lot, see?

FOOL. And had you opened the shutters, as well as the window?

CAPTAIN. Yes, the shutters too.

FOOL. In December? At midnight, with the thermometer down to below freezing, a damp fog that can turn you to stone? "I'm suffocating, quick, some fresh air! What do we care if we all come down with pneumonia?" Did you have your coats on, at least?

CAPTAIN. No, just our jackets.

FOOL. Casual elegance!

CAPTAIN. But I can assure you, it wasn't cold at all.

CHIEF. No, it wasn't cold . . .

FOOL. Oh yeah? On that night the weather report listed temperatures that would petrify a polar bear all over Italy, and they weren't cold. On the contrary— "springtime!" Do you guys have a personal African monsoon that passes through here every night, or is it the "gulf stream current" coming up "Saint Mark's tunnel" and passing along underground through the sewer system?

CAPTAIN. Excuse me, your honor, but I don't understand; awhile ago you said you were here deliberately to help us, but in fact all you're doing is calling every one of our statements into question. Mocking us, humiliating us . . .

FOOL. All right, maybe I am exaggerating, questioning too much. But here you feel as though you're looking at one of those games for retarded morons that appears in the Sunday comic page: "find the thirty-seven errors and contradictions of Inspector Dopey Dum-dum." And how can I help you? (*The policeman sit down, discouraged and silent.*) All right, all right, don't pull those long faces. Cheer up! I promise that from this moment on I won't poke fun at you anymore. The proceedings will be absolutely serious! Now, let's forget about what led up to the event—

CHIEF. Yes, let's forget it.

FOOL. And get down to the event itself: the jump.

CAPTAIN. Agreed.

FOOL. Our anarchist friend, overcome by raptus . . . let's see if together we can find a slightly more credible reason for this mad act. He leaps to his feet, takes a run—just a second, who served as his "footstool?"

CAPTAIN. What? The "footstool?"

FOOL. In other words, which one of you stood next to the window with the fingers of both hands interlocked at the height of his stomach: like this. For him to put his foot on —and then, wham!, a blow that lifts him in flight over the ledge.

CAPTAIN. What in the world are you saying, your honor; do you think that we—

FOOL. No, for heaven's sake, don't get upset. I was just asking . . . thinking that, since it's a fairly high jump, with so little space for the preliminary run, with no outside help . . . I wouldn't want anybody to be able to question—

CAPTAIN. No, there's nothing to question, your honor, I assure you; he did it all by himself!

FOOL. Wasn't there even the kind of little stool they use in competitions?

CAPTAIN. No . . .

FOOL. Maybe the jumper was wearing shoes with elastic heels!

CAPTAIN. No, no elastic heels.

FOOL. Well, then let's see what we have. On the one hand, a man about five foot ten, alone, with no help, and without a ladder. On the other hand, half a dozen cops who were standing only a few yards away — one of them right next to the window, in fact — and yet don't make it in time to stop him . . .

CAPTAIN. But it happened so suddenly!

OFFICER. And you have no idea how quick that devil was. I just barely managed to grab him by a foot.

FOOL. Aha! You see, my provocation technique works: you grabbed him by the foot!

OFFICER. Yes, but the shoe stayed in my hand, and he went down anyway.

FOOL. It doesn't matter. What matters is that the shoe stayed behind. That shoe proves beyond the slightest doubt that you tried to save him!

CAPTAIN. Of course, it's beyond all doubt.

CHIEF. (*to the OFFICER*) Good for you!

OFFICER. Thanks, Chief, I'm —

CHIEF. Shut up!

FOOL. Just a moment . . . something's out of whack here. (*shows the officers a piece of paper*) Did the suicide victim have three shoes?

CHIEF. What do you mean, three shoes?

FOOL. Just that. One of them apparently remained in the hands of the policeman, as he himself testified a couple of days after the unfortunate event. (*shows the paper*) It's right here.

CAPTAIN. Yes, that's true. He told a reporter that.

FOOL. But here, in this other attached report, everybody insists that as the anarchist lay dying on the courtyard pavement, he still had both shoes on. All the eye-witnesses who gathered around testify to it, including a columnist from *l'Unitá* and other reporters who happened to be on the scene.

CAPTAIN. I don't see how that could have happened.

FOOL. Neither do I! Unless this speedy officer managed to race down the stairs, arrive in time to reach the second-floor landing, stick his head out the window before the suicide passed him on the way down, place his shoe back on his foot as he flew by, and zip like lightning back up to the fourth floor at the very instant the falling man hit the ground.

CHIEF. There, you see, you're acting sarcastic again!

FOOL. You're right. I can't resist it . . . forgive me. Now then: three shoes—excuse me, would you happen to remember if he was a triped, by any chance?

CHIEF. What?

FOOL. If the railroad worker, the suicide victim, had three feet. In which case it would have been logical for him to wear three shoes.

CHIEF. (*irritated*) No, he was not a triped!

FOOL. Please, don't get mad. Especially since you can expect even worse than that from an anarchist!

OFFICER. That's a fact!

CHIEF. Shut up!

CAPTAIN. What a mess, for crying outloud. We'd better find a plausible explanation, otherwise—

FOOL. I've got it!

CHIEF. What's that?

FOOL. Here it is: Obviously one of his shoes was a little big for him. Therefore, not having an innersole on hand, he put on another, narrower shoe before putting on the large one.

CAPTAIN. Two shoes on the same foot?

FOOL. Sure, what's so strange about that? Like galoshes, remember? Those rubber overshoes they used to wear . . .

CHIEF. Exactly, used to.

FOOL. Well, some people still wear them. In fact, you know what I think? That what was left in the officer's hand wasn't a shoe, but a galosh.

CAPTAIN. Oh no, it's impossible. An anarchist with galoshes! That stuff is for old-fashioned types, conservatives —

FOOL. Anarchists are very conservative. At any rate, if you're not satisfied with either the galoshes or the story of the three shoes — ( *The telephone rings. Everyone stops. The INSPECTOR picks up the receiver.* )

CAPTAIN. Excuse me. ( *into the phone* ) Yes, what is it? Just a minute. ( *to the CHIEF* ) It's the guard. He says there's a newspaper woman downstairs at the door who wants to see you, Chief.

CHIEF. Oh, that's right; I made an appointment with her for today . . . she's from *l'Expresso* or *l'Europeo*, I can't remember which. Ask if her name is Feletti.

CAPTAIN. ( *into the phone* ) Is her name Feletti? ( *to the CHIEF* ) Yes, Maria Feletti.

CHIEF. Then she's the one. She wanted an interview. Please ask her to come by some other time; I really can't make it today —

FOOL. No indeed! I wouldn't dream of having you change your plans on my account!

CHIEF. How do you mean?

FOOL. I know that one; she's an important woman, and she could take it the wrong way. She's very touchy! If she's miffed, she wouldn't hesitate to write one of those articles about you — show her in, for heaven's sake!

CHIEF. But what about your investigation?

FOOL. It can wait. Don't you understand yet that I'm in the same boat with you guys? People like her you have to try to get on your side, not against you! Take it from me.

CHIEF. All right (*turning to the CAPTAIN, still holding the phone*) Ask her to come up.

CAPTAIN. (*into the phone*) Show her into my office. (*hangs up*)

CHIEF. And what will you do; are you going to leave us?

FOOL. I wouldn't dream of it. I never abandon my friends, especially in moments of danger!

CAPTAIN AND CHIEF. You're staying?

CHIEF. And how are you going to present yourself? Do you want that vulture of a newspaperwoman to find out who you are and what you're here for? So that she can go ahead and spread it all over her paper? In that case you might as well say you want to see us wiped out!

FOOL. No, I don't want to see you wiped out. Don't worry; the vulture will never find out who I really am.

CAPTAIN. No? But how—

FOOL. Absolutely not. I'll change my identity. For me it's child's play, believe me—psychiatrist, inspector from the criminal division, head of *Interpol*, chief of the scientific division: take your choice. If the vulture should try to embarrass you with some sneaky question, all you have to do is throw me a wink and I'll intervene. The important thing is that you don't compromise yourselves . . . you—

CHIEF. That's awfully generous of you, your honor. (*squeezes his hands with motion*)

FOOL. Don't go on calling me judge, for pity's sake! From this moment on, I am Marcantonio Banzi Piccinni; from the scientific division. All right?

CAPTAIN. But there really is a Captain Banzi Piccinni, down in Rome —

FOOL. Exactly. That way, if the reporter writes something we don't like, it will be easy to show that she invented the whole thing by calling the real Captain Piccinni from Rome as a witness.

CAPTAIN. Wow, you're a genius! Do you really think you can play the part of the captain?

FOOL. Don't worry; during the last war I was a chaplain for the Green Berets.

CHIEF. Quiet, she's here.

(*The REPORTER enters.*)

CHIEF. Come right in, ma'am.

REPORTER. Good evening. I'd like to see the Chief, please.

CHIEF. That's me, ma'am; pleased to meet you. We've only spoken on the phone, unfortunately.

REPORTER. How do you do. The guard down at the door gave me a bit of trouble.

CHIEF. You're right; please excuse the inconvenience. It was my fault for neglecting to inform him that you were coming. I'd like to introduce my assistants: Officer Pisani; the Captain in charge of this office . . .

REPORTER. Pleased to meet you.

CAPTAIN. My Pleasure, ma'am. (*shakes her hand with military vigor*)

REPORTER. Good Lord, what a grip!

CAPTAIN. I'm sorry.

CHIEF. (*indicating the FOOL, who is messing about with his back turned*) And finally, the other Captain . . . Captain?!

FOOL. Here I am (*He appears with a false mustache, a*

*black patch over one eye, and one hand wearing a brown glove. The astonished CHIEF is unable to continue, so the FOOL introduces himself.*) Captain Marcantoni Banzi Piccinni, of the Scientific Division. Please excuse my stiff hand; it's wood, a souvenir of the Nicaraguan campaign, ex-advisor to the Contras. Have a seat, ma'am.

CHIEF. Can I offer you a drink?

REPORTER. No thanks. If you don't mind, I'd prefer to begin right away; I'm in a bit of a hurry. Unfortunately, I have to hand in the article this evening; it goes to the typographer tonight.

CHIEF. All right, as you wish. Let's get started at once; we're ready.

REPORTER. I'd like to ask a number of questions. (*Takes out a note pad and reads.*) The first is actually directed to you, Inspector, and forgive me if it's a little provocative . . . If it's all right with you, I'll use the tape recorder—unless you're opposed to it (*takes a tape recorder out of her purse*).

CAPTAIN. Well, to tell the truth, we—

FOOL. Heavens no, go right ahead. (*to the INSPEC-TOR*) First rule: never contradict.

CAPTAIN. But if we let something escape . . . and want to deny it later, she has the proof . . .

REPORTER. Excuse me, is anything wrong?

FOOL. (*with perfect timing*) No, no, on the contrary. The Captain was just praising you; he says you're a very courageous woman, of real democratic principles . . . a lover of truth and justice, whatever they may cost!

REPORTER. That's awfully kind of him.

CAPTAIN. What would you like to ask?

REPORTER. Why do they call you window-riding instructor?

CAPTAIN. Window-riding instructor? Me?

REPORTER. Yes, or also "Captain riding instructor."

CAPTAIN. And who supposedly calls me that?

REPORTER. I have here the photocopy of a letter from a young anarchist, sent from the San Vittore prison where the boy was being held during the very time of our anarchist's death. The letter talks about you, Inspector . . . and about this room.

CAPTAIN. Oh, really? And what does it say?

REPORTER. (*reads*) "The Inspector from the fourth-floor office forced me to sit astride the window ledge with my legs hanging down, and then started poking and insulting me . . . 'jump; why don't you jump . . . don't have the guts, eh? Finish it off! What are you waiting for?' I swear I had to clench my teeth so I wouldn't give in, so I wouldn't let myself go."

FOOL. (*as Piccinni*) Wonderful! Sounds like a scene from a Hitchcock movie.

REPORTER. If you don't mind, Captain, my question was directed to the head of this office, not to you. (*placing the microphone in front of the CAPTAIN's mouth*) How would you respond to this?

FOOL. (*in the CAPTAIN's ear*): Calm and indifferent!

CAPTAIN. I have no response at all. You answer me, instead, very frankly: do you think I forced the railroad worker into a riding position also?

FOOL. Ssh; don't get caught. (*pretending to sing to himself*) the vulture's flying high, way up in the sky, far away from my house . . .

REPORTER. Am I mistaken, Captain, or are you attempting to disrupt this conversation?

FOOL. Not at all, I was only commenting. And if you'll allow me, Miss Feletti, I'd like to ask you if you think we write commercials for Windex, since you seem absolutely determined to find us doing a window-test with every anarchist we can get our hands on?!

REPORTER. Needless to say, Captain, you're very clever.

CAPTAIN. (*to the FOOL*) Thanks, you got me out of a really tight spot. (*slaps him on the shoulder*)

FOOL. Go easy with the hands, Inspector; I have a glass eye! (*points to his black patch*)

CAPTAIN. A glass eye?

FOOL. And watch out when you shake my hand, too; it's artificial.

REPORTER. Getting back to the subject of windows, the report on the parabola of the fall seems to be missing from the judge's dossier—the one containing his decision to close the inquiry.

CHIEF. Parabola of the fall?

REPORTER. Yes, the parabola of the alleged suicide's fall to the ground.

CHIEF. What's the purpose of that report?

REPORTER. Its purpose is to establish whether or not the anarchist was still completely alive at the moment when he flew out of the window. That is, if he had taken the slightest jump before he went out, or if he fell like an inanimate object, as the report in fact states, grazing the wall. If any fractures or lesions were found on his arms or hands, which according to the report was not the case— in other words, the alleged suicide did not throw his hands forward to protect himself at the moment of impact with the ground: a normal and totally instinctive gesture.

CAPTAIN. Yes, but don't forget that we're dealing with a suicide here—a person who threw himself out because he wanted to die!

FOOL. Ah, but that doesn't mean—unfortunately, I

have to back up Miss Feletti on this point. As you see, I'm completely objective. All sorts of experiments have been done on the subject; they've taken suicides and thrown them out of windows, and in each case they noticed that, instinctively, at the right moment, they all threw their hands forward: smack!

CHIEF. Great help you're giving us! Are you crazy?

FOOL. Yes, how did you find out?

REPORTER. But the most disconcerting detail, for which I would really like an explanation, concerns a tape recording that's missing from that same file on the judge's decision to close the inquiry. The tape recorded the exact time of the phone call for the ambulance. The call was placed through the switchboard of police head-quarters, and the Red Cross attendant, as well as the telephone operator, testified that it was made at two minutes to twelve. But every reporter who came running into the courtyard swears that the jump occurred at exactly three minutes after twelve. In short, the stretcher was summoned five minutes before the anarchist flew out of the window. Can any of you explain this curious fact?

FOOL. Oh, we often call for stretchers, just in case, because you never know . . . and sometimes we hit it at just the right minute, as you see.

CAPTAIN. (*giving him a whap on the shoulder*) Great!

FOOL. Careful, my eye—it may pop out!

CHIEF. Anyway, I don't understand what you're trying to accuse us of. Is it some kind of crime to be prepared? Barely three minutes ahead of time—come on, you know that for the police being ahead of time is all-important!

CAPTAIN. Besides, I'm thoroughly convinced that the

fault lies with the watches. Those reporters' watches must have been slow . . . I mean fast . . .

CHIEF. Or maybe the operator who tape-recorded our call had a slow time-clock . . .

OFFICER. Sure, more than likely.

REPORTER. Strange timepiece disease!

FOOL. What's so strange about it? We're not in Switzerland, here. Every one of us sets his watch at the time he likes best. Some people prefer being early, others late . . . this is a nation of artists, incredible individualists, rebels against habit —

CAPTAIN. Great, fantastic! (*whaps him on the shoulder; clicking sound of glass marble hopping along the floor*)

FOOL. You see?! What did I tell you . . . you knocked out my glass eye!

CAPTAIN. (*going down on his hands and knees to look for it*) I'm sorry . . . we'll find it for you right away.

FOOL. Good thing I have the eye-patch that held it back; otherwise, who knows where it would have wound up. Excuse me, ma'am, what were we talking about?

REPORTER. About the fact that we're a nation of artists who like to rebel against habit. And I agree with you there — judges who order investigations to be closed are the most rebellious of all: they forget to gather eyewitness reports, tapes with the record of times, data about the fall; they neglect to inquire how come an ambulance stretcher was called ahead of time — all petty details! Including the bruises at the base of the dead man's neck: their cause is anything but clear.

CHIEF. Be careful, ma'am. I'd advise you not to go talking at random; it's dangerous.

REPORTER. Is that a threat?

FOOL. No, no, Chief; I don't believe Miss Feletti is talking at random. She's obviously alluding to a version of the facts that I've heard suggested on more than one occasion — and strangely enough, it originated right in the halls of this building.

CHIEF. What's that all about?

FOOL. People are whispering that during the anarchist's last interrogation someone who was there got impatient and, just a few minutes before midnight, landed a huge blow on the neck of the above-mentioned anarchist. Calm down, Chief . . . he was reportedly semi-paralyzed. In addition he was rattling from the throat, because he couldn't breathe. Then the ambulance was called, and in the meantime, while they were trying to revive him, they threw open the window. They carried the anarchist up to the window-sill and let him hang over a little, so the rather cool night air could bring him to. They say two people were holding him . . . and as it often happens in these cases, each one was relying on the other — should I hold him? Do you want to hold him? — and wham-bam, down he went! (*The infuriated IN-SPECTOR strides forward, slips on the glass marble, and crashes to the floor.*)

REPORTER. There, exactly like that!

CHIEF. (*to the FOOL*) For chrissakes, have you gone crazy?

FOOL. That's right, Chief, sixteen times.

INSPECTOR. God damn it! What did I slip on?

FOOL. On my glass eye, that's what! Look, you got it all dirty! Officer, would you mind getting me a glass of water to wash it? (*The OFFICER exits.*)

REPORTER. You have to admit that this version clarifies a whole lot of mysteries: the reason why the stretcher was summoned ahead of time, why the fall was like that of an inanimate body—and even why the District Attorney used such a curious term when he was making his concluding remarks.

FOOL. What term? Please try to be more explicit; I've already got a headache from my own problems.

REPORTER. The D.A. declared in writing that the anarchist's death must be considered "accidental." *Accident*, mind you, not *suicide* as you gentlemen called it. And there's a big difference between the two terms. On the other hand, the way the Captain described the incident, it would be possible to define it precisely as an "accident." (*In the meantime the OFFICER, who has returned with the glass of water, hands it to the FOOL. Entirely absorbed in the woman's speech, the FOOL swallows the glass marble as if it were a pill.*)

FOOL. Oh my god! The eye! Good grief, I've swallowed the eye—oh well at least I hope it cures my headache.

CHIEF. (*in the ear of the false CAPTAIN*) What kind of game are you playing now?

CAPTAIN. (*alternating with the CHIEF*) Don't you think you've given that vulture a little too much rope? At this point she's sure she can hang us!

FOOL. Please, let me handle it. (*to the REPORTER*) Still, I can prove to you ma'am, that this last version is completely unreliable.

REPORTER. Unreliable, sure; just like the testimonies of the pensioners were considered unreliable by the judge who ordered the case to be closed!

FOOL. What's this story about unreliable pensioners?

REPORTER. It's odd that you haven't been informed about it! In his decision to close the inquiry, this judge declared that the testimonies of the three customers cited by our anarchists were unreliable. The men asserted that they had spent the tragic afternoon of the bombing playing cards with him in a tavern down by the canal.

FOOL. The testimonies were unreliable? Why?

REPORTER. Because, as the judge explained, "these are elderly people in poor health, and also invalids."

FOOL. Did he write that in his decision, too?

REPORTER. Yes.

FOOL. Well, I don't see how you could really disagree with him. These elderly gentlemen are not terribly wealthy, am I right?

REPORTER. Yes. They are retired factory workers. Quite poor.

FOOL. Well—the judge was quite correct then. Poor people, from my experience, try like hell to forget. If they had to remember even half of what they've gone through, they'd find a nice window for themselves four floors up. That's assuming they're not in one of those new housing projects where the windows don't open. Interesting architecture—saved the lives of a lot of poor people. As for being sick, well—have you seen what they eat—it's disgusting. Some of them only eat cheese that the government gives them. Now is that a balanced diet?

REPORTER. Ha ha, that's too much! Well apart from the grotesque comedy, should the blame be placed on them, if they're reduced to such a state?

FOOL. No, it's society that's definitely at fault! But we're not here to put capitalism and the bosses on trial, we're here to talk about which witnesses are more reliable and which ones less! If somebody is in bad shape because he's been exploited too long or had an accident in the factory, we, as representatives of order and justice, should not become involved.

CHIEF. Good for you, Captain!

FOOL. You don't have the means to provide yourself with sufficient vitamins, proteins, sugars, fats and minerals to make your memory work? Well then, too bad for you; as a judge, I turn you down — but you're out of the game, a second-class citizen.

REPORTER. Aha, you see! I knew that sooner or later we'd get down to the question of class, and of class privilege!

FOOL. So, who ever denied it? Sure, I'll admit it, it's true: ours is a society divided into classes — and that goes for witnesses, too: there are first, second, third, and fourth-class witnesses. It's never a question of age. I mean, for god's sake, who's kidding who? Why does somebody bother getting a college degree? And afterwards, why does he become a privileged stockholder? So that he can receive the same treatment as a crummy pensioner? And they say that in Italy nobody has faith in the dollars anymore! Age has nothing to do with it. America's most trusted official is a septagenarian President who can't even remember the words to America the Beautiful. He reads the lyrics from a cue card and his wife whispers into his ear. It would be a tragedy if he were an actor. But somehow it just makes people trust him more. ( *The FOOL-CAPTAIN comes out from behind the desk, and we discover that he has a wooden leg, like a pirate's. All stare at him dumb-founded. He comments imperturbably.* ) Operation Cobra. Nasty souvenir! But no point talking about it; it's water under the bridge.

(*The door opens, and INSPECTOR BERTOZZO looks in. He has a bandage over one eye.*)

BERTOZZO. Excuse me, am I interrupting?
CHIEF. Come in, come in, Inspector Bertozzo. Please sit down.

BERTOZZO. I just had to deliver this. (*shows a small metal box*)

CHIEF. What is it?

BERTOZZO. A facsimile of the bomb that exploded in the bank.

REPORTER. Oh my god!

BERTOZZO. Don't worry, ma'am, it's defused.

CHIEF. Well, then, put it down right over there . . . now, be a nice guy and shake hands with your colleague. You too, Inspector . . . come here and patch things up.

BERTOZZO. Patch what up, Chief? I would at least like to know what made him fly off the handle and give me this shiner! (*The CHIEF elbows him in the ribs.*)

CAPTAIN. Oh, you don't know, eh? And what about the razzberry?

BERTOZZO. What razzberry?

CHIEF. Come on, that's enough! There are strangers present.

FOOL. Quite so.

BERTOZZO. But Chief, I'm just trying to understand what got into him. He comes in without even saying hello, and—bam!

FOOL. Well, he could have at least said hello to him. He's right about that, after all!

BERTOZZO. There, you see—excuse me, but you look so familiar.

FOOL. Must be because we're both wearing an eye-patch. (*All laugh.*)

BERTOZZO. No, really, joking aside—

FOOL. Please allow me: I am Captain Marcantonio Banzi Piccinni, of the Scientific Division.

BERTOZZO. Piccinni? But you can't—it's not possible—I know Captain Piccinni . . .

CHIEF. (*deftly kicking him*) No, you don't know him.

BERTOZZO. I don't know him? You must be kidding!

CAPTAIN. No, you do not know him (*kick*).

BERTOZZO. Listen, don't you start up again—

CHIEF. Forget the whole thing. (*kick*).

BERTOZZO. But we went through the Police Academy together! (*receives another kick, this time from the FOOL.*)

FOOL. We're telling you to forget the whole thing! (*gives him a slap as well*)

BERTOZZO. Hey, what do you think you're—

FOOL. (*pointing to the Captain*) It was him. (*The CHIEF pulls him aside, toward the REPORTER.*)

CHIEF. If you'll allow me, Inspector, I'd like to introduce Miss—I'll explain to you later—Miss Feletti, the reporter. Now do you catch on? (*digs him with an elbow*)

BERTOZZO. Pleased to meet you. I'm Inspector Bertozzo . . . No, I don't catch on (*Kick from the CHIEF and another from the FOOL, who is beginning to enjoy it so much that he kicks the CHIEF too. At the same time, he lands a robust slap on the back of both BERTOZZO's and the INSPECTOR's necks, simultaneously. Convinced that it was the CAPTAIN:*) You see, Chief, I told you; he's the one who always starts! . . . (*To conclude, the FOOL slaps the REPORTER on the rear and then points to the CHIEF.*)

REPORTER. I beg your pardon, just what do you think you're doing?!

CHIEF. (*thinking she is referring to the squabble*) You're right, but I don't know how to explain it. Bertozzo, cut it out and listen to me! The lady is here for a very important interview understand? (*kicks him, also winking at him conspiratorially*)

BERTOZZO. I understand.

CHIEF. So, ma'am, if you'd care to, you can ask him some questions too. The Inspector is a specially trained expert in ballistics and explosives.

REPORTER. Oh, yes, there is something you could clear up for me. You said that that box contains the facsimile of the bank bomb.

BERTOZZO. Well, it's a very rough facsimile, since all the original explosive devices were lost, so to speak . . .

REPORTER. But one of the bombs was saved, unexploded.

BERTOZZO. That's right, the one that was left in the Bank of Commerce.

REPORTER. Then explain to me why it is that, instead of defusing it and handing it over to the Scientific Division, as they usually do, so that it could be thoroughly examined, the minute they found it they brought it into a courtyard, buried it and blew it up?

BERTOZZO. Excuse me, how come you want to know that?

REPORTER. You know why as well as I do, Inspector. That way, the "signature" of the murderers was destroyed along with the bomb.

FOOL. It's true, as the saying goes, "tell me how you put together a bomb and I'll tell you who you are."

BERTOZZO. ( *shaking his head* ) No, sir, that sure isn't Piccinni! ( *The FOOL has grabbed the box containing the bomb.* )

CHIEF. Of course it isn't! Shut up!

BERTOZZO. Ah, I didn't think so. Who is it, then? ( *receives another kick* )

FOOL. If Inspector Bertozzo will allow me, as head of the Scientific Division —

BERTOZZO. Who's supposed to buy that? What are

you doing? Please, let go of that box; it's dangerous!

FOOL. (*swiftly kicks him*) I'm from the Scientific Division. Move over there.

CHIEF. But, are you really familiar with those things? (*The FOOL looks at him disdainfully.*)

FOOL. You see, ma'am, a bomb of this type is so complex . . . look at the number of wires, two detonators, the timing device, primer, springs, levers—as I said, it's so complex that one could very easily hide a double mechanism with delayed explosion so that nobody could find it, unless they dismantled the entire bomb piece by piece—which would take a whole day, believe me!—and in the meantime, boom!

CHIEF. (*to BERTOZZO*) He really does sound like a technician, doesn't he?

BERTOZZO. (*stubborn*) Yes, but he's not Piccinni.

FOOL. That's why they preferred to lose the killers' signature, as you called it, and set the bomb off in a courtyard, rather than risk seeing it blow up in the middle of the public, with a resulting massacre even more horrible than the first. You see?

REPORTER. Yes, this time you really have convinced me.

FOOL. I've even succeeded in convincing myself!

CAPTAIN. I'm convinced too. Good; it was an excellent idea. (*He grasps the FOOL's hand and shakes it hard. The wooden hand comes off and he finds himself holding it limply.*)

FOOL. There, you pulled it off. I told you it was wooden!

CAPTAIN. I'm sorry.

FOOL. Now all you have left to pull off is my leg! (*He screws his hand back on.*)

CHIEF. (*to Bertozzo*) Bertozzo, you say something

too; try to show that we're not asleep in our division, either. (*He gives him an encouraging slap on the shoulder.*)

BERTOZZO. Sure. The real bomb was pretty complex. I saw it. Much more complex than this one. Obviously the work of very highly-trained technicians . . . professionals, as they say . . .

CHIEF. Careful!

REPORTER. Professionals? Military people, perhaps?

BERTOZZO. It's more than likely. (*All three of the others kick him.*)

CHIEF. Goddam jerk!

BERTOZZO. Ow! Why, what did I say?

REPORTER. (*finishes taking notes*) Ah, yes. Right. So even though you were aware of the fact that to construct, not to mention handle, bombs of this sort you have to have the training and experience of professionals— preferably military professionals—in spite of that, as I said, you threw yourselves madly on one single, forlorn anarchist group, completely neglecting all the other leads . . . and I don't have to point out the ideology and political convictions of those other leads!

FOOL. Of course, if you go by Bertozzo's version. But it can't be considered highly reliable, since he isn't a real explosives technician. He's just interested in it as a hobby!

BERTOZZO. (*insulted*) Hobby, nothing! What do you mean, I don't know about it? What the hell do you know about it? Who are you, anyway? (*turning to the two other policemen*) Would you kindly tell me who he is? (*more kicks, forcing him to sit down*)

CHIEF. Keep still.

CAPTAIN. Calm down.

REPORTER. Don't worry, Captain; I'm sure everything he said was true, just as it's true that the entire national police force and legal system rushed to indict — if I may use the expression — the screwiest, most pathetic cluster of kooks anyone can imagine: that anarchist group headed by the dancer!

CHIEF. You're right, they were kooks. But that's the facade they deliberately built up so that they wouldn't attention.

REPORTER. In actual fact, what do you discover behind the facade? You discover that out of the ten people belonging to that group, two were really yours: two confidants, or rather provocateurs and spies. One is a Roman fascist, well-known to everybody except our group of gullible innocents; the other is one of your own police agents also masquerading as an anarchist.

FOOL. Yes, as far as the officer disguised as an anarchist is concerned, I don't understand how they possibly could have believed him. I know the guy: he's such a dodo that if you ask him to describe Bakunin, he'll tell you it's a Swiss cheese without holes!

BERTOZZO. (*aside*) I could kill that guy. He seems to know everything and everybody . . . But I could swear I know him!

CHIEF. I completely disagree with you, Captain: that officer-informant of ours is an excellent agent! Very highly trained!

REPORTER. And have you got many more of these highly trained officer-informants sprinkled here and there among the various far-left groups?

FOOL. (*sing-song*) "The vulture's flying high . . . "

CHIEF. Madam, intelligence gathering is the backbone of every civilized nation.

FOOL. And even a few uncivilized ones.

CHIEF. Without proper intelligence a free nation

throws itself on the mercy of every instigator, every radical movement.

FOOL. Every election.

CHIEF. I for one feel not the slightest embarrassment that we, the government, are using every tool we can think of . . .

FOOL. And a few we've only dreamed of.

REPORTER. Oh, now you're just bluffing, Chief.

CHIEF. Not at all. Even tonight, in the audience, I guarantee there are a few of our men, as always . . . do you want to see? (*Claps his hands sharply; several VOICES respond from different places in the theater*).

VOICES. Yessir! Ready, Chief! At your orders!

FOOL. (*laughing and turning to the audience*) Don't worry, those are just actors. The real agents are out there too, sitting tight and keeping their mouths shut.

CHIEF. You see? At ease at ease. Our strength lies in our confidants and informers.

CAPTAIN. They're needed to warn us about what's going to happen, check things out . . .

FOOL. Provoke terrorist attacks so that later they'll have a pretext for carrying out repressive actions . . . (*The officers turn toward him with shocked suddenness.*) I just wanted to get the jump on the remark the lady was obviously about to make.

REPORTER. Yes, quite obviously! At any rate, if they had every member of that little pilgrim band under total and continuous surveillance, how come the band was able to organize such a complicated attack, without your coming in to stop them?

FOOL. Watch out, the vulture's getting ready to dive!

CHIEF. The fact is that during that period our informer-agent was absent from the group.

FOOL. It's true, he even brought an excuse note signed by his parents!

CAPTAIN. Please! (*under his breath*) Your honor . . .

REPORTER. But what about the other confidant, the fascist? He was there, wasn't he? So much so, that the Roman judge holds him mainly responsible for organizing and fomenting the attack. In the judge's words, he took advantage of the anarchists' simple-mindedness to make them carry out a terrorist act, while they had no idea of its criminal nature. These are the words and opinions of the judge, you understand.

FOOL. Bang, the vulture has landed!

CHIEF. First of all, I can tell you that the fascist you're referring to is definitely not one of our confidants.

REPORTER. Then how come he was always hanging around central headquarters, especially the political division, in Rome?

CHIEF. If you say so . . . that's not my understanding.

FOOL. (*extending his hand to the CHIEF*) Good, an excellent parry! (*The CHIEF shakes his wooden hand, which remains in his own.*)

FOOL. (*indifferently*) Oh, it's all right, you can keep it. I have another one (*takes out a second, this time a feminine, wooden hand*)

CAPTAIN. But it's for a woman!

FOOL. No, it's unisex. (*screws it on*)

REPORTER. (*who in the meantime has taken several sheets of paper out of a small briefcase*) Ah, that's not your understanding? Then I suppose it's also not your understanding that out of 173 dynamite attacks that have been carried out until today—twelve each month, one every three days—out of 173 attacks, as I said 173 attacks, as I said, a good 102 of them (*reading from document*) were found to have been definitely organized by fascists. Once in a while you discover that there are several different secret services behind these attacks; they come from the East and from the West: France, America, Italy, Israel and even the Vatican. Investigating the bombs in the Rome airport, we found that the CIA knew about them far in advance of the event.

FOOL. (*waving his wooden hand like a fan under his chin, in a gesture of disbelief*) Incredible!

CHIEF. Yes, those figures should be considered more or less accurate indications . . . What do you think, Inspector?

CAPTAIN. I'd have to verify them, but in general I think they coincide with our own.

REPORTER. Uh-huh. And if you have time one of these days, why not also try verifying how many of these attacks were organized with the intention of casting suspicion and responsibility on far-left groups.

CAPTAIN. Well, almost all of them . . . that's obvious.

REPORTER. Yes, that's obvious. And how many times have you fallen for it — more or less naively?

FOOL. (*still rotating the woman's hand around his face*) Ooh, you're mean!

CHIEF. When it comes to that, quite a few labor leaders and several Communist Party officials have also fallen for it, more or less naively. Look, I have an article right here, from *l'Unità*, which accuses them of "foolishly ambitious and adventuristic leftism" — for an act of vandalism that it later turned out those subversives had absolutely nothing to do with.

REPORTER. I know it: it was a right-wing newspaper that started circulating those rumors, using the customary slogan, "clash of opposite extremes." It always works — for you, too!

FOOL. Viper!

BERTOZZO. But I could swear I know him! I've got to tear off his eye-patch!

FOOL. (*sarcastically interceding*) Well, what did you expect, ma'am? That we would respond to your obvious provocations by admitting that if we in the police force had bothered to seriously follow up other, more reliable leads, like paramilitary and fascist organizations financed by big industrialists, led and supported by military officers from Greece and surrounding territories, instead of going on a goose-chase after that handful of raggedy-ass anarchists, maybe we would have gotten to the bottom of the whole mess?

CHIEF. (*to BERTOZZO, who is practically in a frenzy*) Don't worry; I'm about to turn the tables on him all of a sudden. That's his own technique; I'm familiar with it by now! Jesuit dialectics!

FOOL. If that's what you think, I'll tell you you're right. If we had taken this other route, something really big would have hit the fan — Ha, ha!

BERTOZZO. Boy, that's some Jesuit dialectics, all right!

CHIEF. (*to the FOOL*) Have you gone crazy?

BERTOZZO. (*struck by a sudden illumination*) Crazy? (*It clicks.*) The crazy nut — that's who he is!! It's him!

REPORTER. I must admit that, coming from a policeman, such statements are definitely . . . disconcerting!

BERTOZZO. (*pulling at the CHIEF's sleeve*) Chief, I've found out who that guy is; I know him.

CHIEF. Well, keep it to yourself; don't go blabbing it all over. (*He leaves BERTOZZO in the lurch, and goes over to join the FOOL and REPORTER.*)

BERTOZZO. (*drawing the CAPTAIN to one side*) I swear to you, I know that guy. He's never been in the police; he's wearing a disguise.

CAPTAIN. I know it, you're not telling me anything

new. But don't let the Reporter here you.

BERTOZZO. But he's a maniac, don't you understand?

CAPTAIN. You're the maniac, since you won't let me hear a word they're saying! Keep quiet!

FOOL. (*who has been conversing animatedly, in the meantime, with the other two, continues his speech*) Of course, you're a journalist, and you would take to that sort of scandal like a duck to water. You'd only feel a little uneasy, on discovering that that massacre of the innocents in the bank had served the exclusive purpose of burying the conflicts that arose during the "hot autumn" . . . of creating the kind of tension apt to incite the citizens, who are disgusted and outraged at all this subversive criminality, to demand the installation of an authoritarian regime themselves! I don't remember if I read that in *l'Unitá* or *The Struggle Continues*.

BERTOZZO. (*sneaks up behind the FOOL's back and tears off the band holding his eyepatch in place*) There, you see! His eye isn't missing; he still has it!

CHIEF. For god's sake, have you lost your mind?! Of course he has it! Why shouldn't he have it?

BERTOZZO. Why was he wearing the patch, then, if his eye isn't missing?

CAPTAIN. But yours isn't missing, either, underneath that bandage—and nobody's trying to tear it off you!

REPORTER. Oh, how amusing—did you wear the patch just on a whim?

FOOL. No, so that nobody would catch my eye. (*laughs*)

REPORTER. Ha, Ha! That's good. But go on, tell me a little about the scandal that would have erupted.

FOOL. Oh, yes, an enormous scandal . . . lots of arrests on the right, several trials . . . all kinds of big shots compromised: senators, members of parliament, colonels . . . the Social Democrats weep and wail, *Corriere della sera* changes its editor . . . the left demands that the fascist organizations be declared illegal — answer: we'll see . . . the head of the police department is praised for courageous operation, and then retired from the force.

CHIEF. No, Captain . . . those conclusions, you don't mind my saying so, are a little gratuitous.

REPORTER. In this case, I go along with you, Chief, I believe that kind of a scandal would bring greater prestige to the police. It would make the citizens feel they lived in a better state, with a system of justice that was a little less unjust.

FOOL. Naturally — and it would be more than sufficient! Do people demand a really just system? Well, we'll arrange it so that they'll be satisfied with one that's a little less unjust. The workers cry out, "let's put an end to this shameful, animal exploitation" — and we'll see to it mainly that they don't feel ashamed anymore, as long as they keep on being exploited. They would like not to get killed in the factory any longer, so we'll install a few more protective devices, raise the survivor's benefits a little more. They want to see class society eliminated — and we'll work things out so that class differences aren't so huge; or rather, they won't be so visible! They want a revolution, and we'll give them reforms — lots of reforms; we'll drown them in reforms. Or rather, we'll drown them with promises of reforms, because we'll never give them real ones, either!!

CAPTAIN. You know who he reminds me of? Marrone, that judge who's on trial for slandering the court.

CHIEF. No, no; this one is worse — he's completely crazy!

BERTOZZO. Of course he is; I've been trying to tell you that for an hour!

FOOL. You see, the average citizen doesn't stand to

gain anything from the disappearance of dirty deals. No, he's satisfied to see them denounced, to see a scandal break out so that people can talk about it. For him, that's real freedom and the best of all possible worlds — hallelujah!

BERTOZZO. (*grasping and shaking the FOOL's wooden leg*) Look here, look at his leg — can't you see it's fake?

FOOL. Of course it is. It's made of walnut, to be exact.

CHIEF. We can all see that.

BERTOZZO. But it's all a trick; it's tied to his knee! (*tries to unbuckle the straps*)

CAPTAIN. Let him go, you stupid fool! Are you trying to take him apart?

FOOL. No, leave him alone. Let him go ahead and unbuckle me. Thanks; my whole thigh was beginning to prickle.

REPORTER. Oh, for goodness' sake, why are you always interrupting him? You think you'll manage to discredit him in my eyes simply because he doesn't have a wooden leg?

BERTOZZO. No, it's to show you he's a bragging wind-bag, a "hypocritomaniac," that he's never been either mutilated or a captain . . .

REPORTER. Who is he, then?

BERTOZZO. He's just — (*The CHIEF, POLICE OF-FICER and CAPTAIN all rush over to him, gag him and pull him away.*)

CHIEF. Excuse me, ma'am, but he's wanted on the phone. (*They push him down into a chair by the desk, and stick the telephone receiver against his mouth.*)

CAPTAIN. (*into his ear*) You dumb jerk, do you want to ruin us? (*On the right-hand side, the REPORTER and FOOL continue chatting without paying attention to the group of policemen.*)

CHIEF. Don't you understand it's got to be kept secret? If the woman finds out about the counter-investigation, we're done for!

BERTOZZO. What counter-investigation? (*The receiver is again pushed up against his mouth.*) Hello?

CAPTAIN. You're telling me you don't know? Well then how come you kept yammering about knowing everything, when you're completely ignorant? You blab on and on, mess up everything—

BERTOZZO. No, I do not mess up everything; I just want to know—

CHIEF. Quiet! (*whacks him on the hand with the receiver*) Keep phoning and shut up!

BERTOZZO. Oww! Hello, who's calling?

REPORTER. (*who has been talking to the FOOL all this time*) Oh, how amusing! You don't have to worry anymore, Chief; the Captain—that is, the ex-Captain, has told me everything!

CHIEF. What did he tell you?

REPORTER. Who he really is!

CAPTAIN AND CHIEF. He told you?

FOOL. Yes, I couldn't go on lying anymore. She had figured it out herself by this time.

CHIEF. But . . . at least you made her promise not to put it in the paper?

REPORTER. Oh, but of course I'm going to put it in! (*reads from her notes*) "At central police headquarters, I met a bishop dressed in laymen's clothing!"

CAPTAIN AND CHIEF. A bishop?

FOOL. Yes, forgive me for keeping it from you. (*With the greatest naturalness he twists his collar around, revealing the classical churchmen's high collar, with a black pectoral.*)

BERTOZZO. (*slapping himself on the forehead*) a bishop, now! You don't believe him, by any chance?

(*The INSPECTOR picks up a large rubber stamp and stuffs it in his mouth.*)

CAPTAIN. We've really had it with you! (*The FOOL has taken out a red skull-cap and placed it on the back of his head. With austere, deliberate movements, he then unbuttons his jacket, revealing a gold and silver baroque cross; and finally puts on his finger a ring with an enormous violet stone.*)

FOOL. Allow me to introduce myself: Father Antonio A. Antonio appointed by the Holy See as liason observer with the Italian police. As you know, the Holy Father in Rome is a man of great understanding, and as the police department is having difficulty being understood these days, he sent me here to express his compassion and to encourage their continuing solidarity.

REPORTER. Police solidarity?

FOOL. (*points to the officers*) One look at them and you have to admit they could use a little. (*He offers his ring to be kissed by the OFFICER, who rushes over and kisses it gluttonously.*)

BERTOZZO. (*after removing pacifier from his mouth*) Oh, no! Oh, no! This is too much; now he's a bishop-cop, no less! (*The INSPECTOR sticks the pacifier back in his mouth and drags him to one side.*)

CAPTAIN. But we know it's all bunk, too! He's turned himself into a bishop on purpose to save us . . . understand?!

BERTOZZO. To save us? Have you gotten a mystical attack? A need to save your soul?

CAPTAIN. Shut up and kiss his ring! (*He forces him to bow his head toward the FOOL's hand. In the meantime, nonchalantly and without imposing it, the FOOL has managed to cow everyone into performing the act of submission.*)

BERTOZZO. No, goddam it! Not the ring! I refuse! You

all must be going crazy! He's infected you! (*The IN-SPECTOR and OFFICER have rapidly prepared some large bandages, which they place without further ado over BERTOZZO's mouth, so as to cover up half his face, from his nose down.*)

REPORTER. Goodness, what's come over him, poor man?

FOOL. An attack, I believe. (*He takes a syringe out of his breviary and gets ready to give him an injection.*) Hold him still, this will certainly do him good. It's a benedictine tranquilizer. (*With the swiftness of a rattle-snake he administers the injection, then takes out the syringe and observes it. To the CHIEF:*) There's a little left; would you like to try some too? (*Without waiting for an answer, he injects him with the agility of a picador. Suffocated lament from the CHIEF.*)

REPORTER. You probably won't believe this your eminence, but a little while ago, when you were talking about scandals and exclaimed, "it's the best of all possible worlds — hallelujah!", I immediately commented — hope you'll pardon my irreverence —

FOOL. Oh, that's quite all right.

REPORTER. I said, "Wow, that sounds like a priest talking!" You're not offended, are you?

FOOL. Why should I be offended? It's true, I really did sound like a priest, which is what I am. (*BERTOZZO has written with a marker, on the back of the president's portrait, "He's a maniac, a nut!" He shows the sign to the others behind the bishop's back.*) On the other hand, when Saint Gregory the Great, who had just been elected pontiff, discovered that certain members of the papal court were attempting to cover up some grave scandals through the use of plots and maneuvers, he grew angry and cried out the famous phrase: "Nolimus aut velimus, omnibus gentibus, justitiam et veritatem . . ."

REPORTER. Please, your eminence; I flunked Latin three times!

FOOL. Of course; well, in short, he said: "Like it or not, I will impose truth and justice; I will do everything humanly possible to make sure that scandals are clamorously exposed; and do not forget that, in the stench of scandal, all authority is submerged. Let scandal be welcomed, for upon it is based the most enduring power of the state!"

REPORTER. How extraordinary! Would you mind writing out the entire quotation for me here? (*The FOOL sets about writing down the statement, which he has obviously freely adapted from Saint Gregory, in the REPORTER's notebook. In the meantime, the INSPECTOR has grabbed the hand-written sign, with the president's portrait on the other side, away from his colleague and torn it up.*)

CHIEF. (*attacking him*) What the hell have you done? Torn up the president's portrait? Don't you know that's against the law? What's gotten into you?

CAPTAIN. (*pointing to BERTOZZO*) But Chief, the things he's been writing . . . !

CHIEF. I may go along with you about a certain mania some people have for writing melodramatic messages to the public—But that's certainly no reason to go ahead and ruin his portrait! You should be ashamed of yourself! (*Behind the bishop, the REPORTER has been rereading and thoughtfully considering the significance of Saint Gregory's dictum.*)

REPORTER. In other words, it appears that even when there is no scandal, it's necessary to invent it, because it's a marvelous way of maintaining power by providing an "escape valve" for the offended conscience of the masses.

FOOL. Certainly, the catharsis which liberates all tension. And you independent journalists insure that this sacred process continues.

REPORTER. Then why does our government go to such lengths to hide its scandals everytime we try to uncover them.

FOOL. Because we're still a developing nation, practically precapitalist. If you want to see what we have to look forward to, take a good look at a more developed country like America. They have a President who falls asleep at press conferences and keeps forgetting which questions he's answering. They ask him about one thing, he answers with something else. Then he contradicts himself, then they tell him what he said before. He says, 'No I must have been mistaken.' But the public has complete faith in him. 'You thought I called you a son of a bitch, but I actually said it's sunny and you're rich.' And then do the people lose confidence in a leader like that? No, they trust him even more. They say, 'Yes, of course it is sunny and I am rich.' And so the stock market keeps going up. It's stronger than it was before. The important thing is to convince people that everything is going fine. America is up to its ears in scandal: The President's advisors are being indicted, but he stands behind them until they're convicted. Right-wing dictators re-invest US aid in New York real estate, and we welcome our money back. The police bomb people out of their houses in Philadelphia, and the mayor convinces them it's a new kind of urban development. A nuclear reactor nearly melts down in Harrisburg, but we congratulate ourselves that Chernobyl was worse.

REPORTER. Meaning that scandals are the breeding-ground of reaction?

FOOL. No, scandals are the fertilizer of Western democracy. Let me say more. Scandal is the antidote to an even worse poison: namely, people's gaining political consciousness. If people become too conscious we are screwed. For example, has the American government, a real democracy, ever imposed any censorship to keep people from finding out about the murder of all the leaders of the black movement, or the massacre of thousands of helpless Vietnamese? Not at all. They don't even hide the fact that they've manufactured enough nerve gas and bombs to destroy the population of the world ten times over. They don't censor these scandals. And rightly so. Because in this way people have the possibility of becoming indignant. Horrified. 'What kind of government is this? Disgusting generals. Assassins.' And they become indignant. And out of the indignation comes a burp. A liberating burp. It's like Alka-Seltzer. But nothing changes.

(*BERTOZZO, who has been crouching in the background all this time, as if to spring, suddenly whips out a gun, points it at the police officers, tears off his gag, and shouts with cold determination*):

BERTOZZO. Hands up! Backs to the wall or I'll shoot!
CAPTAIN. What the — Bertozzo, have you gone crazy?!
BERTOZZO. Hands up, I said. You too, Chief. I tell you I won't hesitate!
REPORTER. Oh my god!
CHIEF. Calm down, Bertozzo!
BERTOZZO. You calm down, Chief, and don't worry. (*He removes a bunch of handcuffs from the desk, gives them to the OFFICER, and orders him to handcuff everyone.*) Go on, hang them to the coat rack, one by one. (*On*

*the back wall there is in fact a raised horizontal rack, to which all the people present are attached, one after the other: one handcuff on one wrist, the other hung on the coatrack.*) And don't look at me like that; pretty soon you'll understand that this was the only way I had left to get you to listen to me. (*to the OFFICER, who is uncertain whether or not to handcuff the REPORTER as well*) Yes, the lady too . . . and you yourself. (*turning to the FOOL*) And you, my sonofabitch friend from the funny farm, can now do me the favor of telling these gentlemen who you really are. Otherwise, since I've had it up to here with you, I'll blast you right between the eyebrows — get it? (*The policemen and REPORTER show signs of resentment against such irreverence, but BERTOZZO cuts them short.*) You be quiet!

FOOL. I'll be glad to, but I'm afraid that perhaps if I tell them like this, out loud, they won't believe me.

BERTOZZO. What's the matter, you want to send them a singing telegram, maybe?

FOOL. No, but it would be sufficient to show them my documents . . . psychiatric clinical record, etc.

BERTOZZO. O.K. Where are they?

FOOL. Over there, in that briefcase.

BERTOZZO. Move, go get them, and no tricks or I'll kill you! (*The FOOL takes out a half dozen booklets and folders.*)

FOOL. Here they are. (*hands them to BERTOZZO*)

BERTOZZO. (*taking them and distributing them among the handcuffed captives, who have their left hands free*) Here you are, folks . . . seeing is believing!

CHIEF. Nooo! An ex-drawing teacher!? On medical disability? Afflicted with visionary paranoia?! But . . . this man is crazy!

BERTOZZO. (*sighing*) I've been telling you that for an hour!

CAPTAIN. (*reading from another file*) Psychiatric hospitals of Imola, Voghera, Varese, Gorizia, Parma — he's been through all of them!

FOOL. Sure, the madmen's grand tour of Italy.

REPORTER. Fifteen electric shock treatments . . . twenty days in the isolation ward . . . three attacks of vandalism . . .

POLICE OFFICER. (*reading from a document*) pyromaniac! Ten cases of arson!

REPORTER. Let me see. Set fire to the library of Alexandria. Alexandria, Egypt! Back in the second century, A.D.!

BERTOZZO. That's impossible; give it here! (*observes the document*) But he added that himself, in his own handwriting . . . you see! From Egypt up to now . . . !

CHIEF. He's a counterfeiter, too . . . as well as a con man, faker, quick-change artist . . . (*to the FOOL, who is sitting there with his large briefcase on his knees, staring absentmindedly in another direction*) Well, I'm going to put you behind bars, for illegal use and false appropriation of civil and ecclesiastical authority!

FOOL. (*mischievously, shaking his head from side to side*) Uh-uh.

BERTOZZO. No way, he's an official nut. I already know the whole story!

REPORTER. It's a shame; I was ready to write such a good article . . . and he's ruined the whole thing!

INSPECTOR. I'll ruin him! Bertozzo, will you please take this handcuff off me?!

BERTOZZO. Great idea, that way you'll really be done for. You ought to know that in this country crazy people are like sacred cows in India — lay a finger on them and they lynch you!

CHIEF. That lousy bum, criminal, idiot . . . passing himself off as a judge . . . the counter-investigation . . . when I think I almost passed out because of him!

FOOL. No, you weren't hit that hard—especially compared to what you're going to feel now! Look here! (*takes out of his briefcase the metal box which BERTOZZO had left sitting on the table*) Count to ten, and we'll all fly up in the air!

BERTOZZO. What the hell do you think you're doing . . . don't be a moron!

FOOL. I'm a nut, not a moron. Watch what you say, Bertozzo, and throw away the gun—otherwise I'll put my finger right here in the "tramptur" and we'll do it quickly.

REPORTER. Oh, god! Madman, please . . . !

CHIEF. Don't fall for it, Bertozzo. The bomb is defused; how can it blow up?

CAPTAIN. Right, don't fall for it!

FOOL. Well, then, Bertozzo, since you know so much about it—even if your grammar is lousy—take a look and see if it's there or not . . . the detonator . . . look, right here—don't you see it? It's an acoustic Longber.

BERTOZZO. (*almost fainting, drops the gun and keys to the handcuffs*) An acoustic Longber? But where did you find it? (*The FOOL picks up the keys and gun.*)

FOOL. I had it with me. (*pointing to the large briefcase*) I have everything in there! Even a tape recorder, that I used to record everything you've said since I walked in here. (*takes out a tape recorder and exhibits it*) Here it is!

CHIEF. And what do you intend to do with it?

FOOL. Make a couple hundred copies and send them all over: political party headquarters, newspapers, cabinet ministers' offices — ha, ha! This will really go over big!

CHIEF. No, you couldn't do a thing like that. You know perfectly well that those statements we made were all falsified and distorted under your provocations, while you were pretending to be a judge!

FOOL. So, who gives a damn? The important thing is that the scandal breaks out — *nolimus aut velimus*! So the Italian people, like the English and Americans, will become democratic and modern; and so they can finally exclaim, "it's true, we're up to our necks in shit, and that's exactly why we walk with our heads held high!"

### THE END

(*Note: This is where one version of the play published in Italian ended. A second, alternative ending follows.*)

### ALTERNATE ENDING

FOOL. ". . . with our heads held high!" He who is aware of what's floating by just under his chin constantly increases in dignity! (*So saying, he handcuffs BER-TOZZO also, and attaches him to the coatrack.*)

CAPTAIN. All right, do what you want, but please, defuse that bomb right now.

FOOL. No, I'm going to leave it here. It will keep you sitting tight until I'm completely out of your grasp. Before I go out, I'll push down this lever, and tiptoe away. In the meantime, you'd better stay put in here, and hold your breath — because if you so much as move to sound the alarm, this place will blow sky-high, and there won't be a scrap of any of you left — not even a button!

(*At that moment, the lights go out.*)

REPORTER. What happened? Who turned out the light?
FOOL. Who did it? Stop kidding around . . . No . . . help!!!

(*We hear a cry, which continues offstage, followed by an explosion, also offstage, as if coming from the courtyard.*)

CHIEF. Jesus Christ, the nut must have thrown the bomb out the window! Will somebody turn on that light?!
CAPTAIN. It must have been a power failure. Bertozzo, you're over there near the switch; try a minute—

(*The light goes on again at that instant, and we see BER-TOZZO with his hand on the switch.*)

CHIEF. Oh! Finally!
BERTOZZO. Whew! Wonder how that happened?
REPORTER. The madman? He's gone?
CAPTAIN. He must have gone out . . .
OFFICER. (*turning the doorknob*) The door is locked!
CAPTAIN. . . . the window!
REPORTER. Oh, look, my wrist is so thin the handcuff slipped off by itself!
CHIEF. That's great for you; wish we were that lucky. Unfortunately, we can't get out, and keys stayed in the madman's pocket! But quick, run over to the window . . .
REPORTER. (*going and looking out*) There's a bunch of people gathered around the poor man. It's terrible; how could it have happened? (*turning to the CHIEF*) Do

you have some statement you'd like to make, Chief? (*She immediately goes back to being a journalist, holding the microphone up in front of him.*)

CHIEF. Well, I had just left the room —

REPORTER. What are you talking about? How could you have gone out if you were handcuffed right here to the rack?

CHIEF. Ah, yes, you're right. I'm so mixed up . . . I was getting confused with the other time.

CAPTAIN. Anyway, you're a witness to that poor guy's fall; we don't bear the slightest guilt or responsibility!

REPORTER. Certainly, tied up, as you were . . . And now I'll also have to reconsider all my notions regarding that other fall.

CAPTAIN AND CHIEF. For heaven's sake, anybody can make a mistake! (*The CHIEF continues.*) I think that in this case the impulsive act can be imputed to "raptus brought about by darkness." That is, the sudden darkness frightened the madman; the only source of light, although very weak, was the window, and he threw himself toward it like a crazed moth, precipitating to the ground.

REPORTER. Of course, it couldn't have happened any other way. I'd better run over to the paper to file the story.

CHIEF. Yes, go ahead, it's quite all right. (*All shake left hands with the REPORTER.*) Good bye.

CAPTAIN. Nice meeting you . . . and if we can help you some other time, always at your service.

BERTOZZO. Good bye, ma'am. (*So saying, he absent-mindedly takes his hand out of the handcuff and offers it to the REPORTER, kisses her hand, and then places his own back into the cuff. The REPORTER notices this and stands there for a moment, perplexed. (The INSPEC-*

*TOR gives him a slap. The REPORTER collects herself.)*

REPORTER. Thanks again, and good bye, all! (*She goes out, turning the key which has remained in the lock.* )

BERTOZZO. Why did you slap me? You think just because she isn't married, I shouldn't have kissed her hand? Boy, you're so nit-picking!

(*The door opens wide, once more revealing the actor who played the role of the FOOL. He now has a very black, bristly beard, a large paunch, and an austere manner. He is carrying a briefcase.*)

BEARDED MAN. Am I interrupting? I'm looking for the Captain's office . . . the first political division.

CHORUS. You again!

CHIEF. But weren't you smashed on the ground . . . ?

OFFICER. What is this guy, a cat?

BERTOZZO. He's put on a false beard and even a false stomach — he's padded himself!

CAPTAIN. This time, I'm going to tear it off your face and stuff it down your throat! (*They attack him, dragging the entire coatrack with them.*)

BEARDED MAN. (*shouting*) For god's sake!!! Just what do you think you're doing?!! (*He literally slams them against the right-hand wall.*)

CAPTAIN. But it isn't artificial!!! Not unless he transplanted every hair, one at a time!

BERTOZZO. Yeah, his stomach is real, too!

CHIEF. Please excuse us; we had you confused with someone else — you look so much like him!

BEARDED MAN. I declare! Are you in the habit of

tearing out handfuls of whiskers and giving pokes in the middle to every judge who comes here for an investigation?

CAPTAIN. Judge, for an investigation?

CHIEF. You're a judge?

BEARDED MAN. Yes, may I ask what is so upsetting about that? I am a judge from the superior council, my name is Antonio Garassiniti, and I'm here to re-open an inquiry into the death of the anarchist. Do you mind if we get started at once? ( *He sits down and takes a number of folders out of his briefcase. All four policemen collapse onto the floor, in sitting positions, naturally knocking over the coatrack to which they are still handcuffed.* )

CHORUS. Yes, yes — let's get started at once!

( *Lights out. Musical interlude.* )

## THE END